Leading Issues in Social Knowledge Management

Edited by

David Gurteen

Leading Issues in Social Knowledge Management
Volume One

First edition 2012

Copyright © 2012 The authors

Disclaimer: While every effort has been made by the editor, authors and the publishers to ensure that all the material in this book is accurate and correct at the time of going to press, any error made by readers as a result of any of the material, formulae or other information in this book is the sole responsibility of the reader. Readers should be aware that the URLs quoted in the book may change or be damaged by malware between the time of publishing and accessing by readers.

Note to readers.
Some papers have been written by authors who use the American form of spelling and some use the British. These two different approaches have been left unchanged.

ISBN: 978-1-908272-38-6

Printed by Good News Digital Books

Published by: Academic Publishing International Limited, Reading, RG4 9AY, United Kingdom, info@academic-publishing.org

Available from www.academic-bookshop.com

Contents

List of Contributors

Aurilla Aurelie Arntzen Bechina, *Buskerud University College, Kongsberg, Norway*

Robert Ayres, *Cranfield University, Shrivenham, United Kingdom*

Thomas Bebensee, *Utrecht University, Department of Information and Computing Sciences, The Netherlands*

Daniela Castrataro, *Intellectual Assets Centre, Glasgow, UK*

Marguerite Cronk, *Harding University, Searcy, Arkansas, USA*

Alan Durrant, *Middlesex University, London, UK*

Alexeis Garcia-Perez, *Coventry University, UK*

Remko Helms, *Utrecht University, Department of Information and Computing Sciences, The Netherlands*

Eli Hustad, *University of Agder, Kristiansand, Norway*

Minna Janhonen, *Finnish Institute of Occupational Health, Work and Society Team, Helsinki, Finland*

Jan-Erik Johanson, *University of Helsinki, Department of Political and Economic Studies, Finland*

Alwyn Lau, *KDU College, Kuala Lumpur, Malaysia*

Vincent Ribiere, *Bangkok University, Bangkok, Thailand*

Marco Spruit, *Utrecht University, Department of Information and Computing Sciences, The Netherlands*

Mustafa Tuncay, *Atatürk Teacher Training Academy, Nicosia, North Cyprus*

Nazime Tuncay, *Near East University, Nicosia, North Cyprus*

Stuart Watson, *Intellectual Assets Centre, Glasgow, UK*

Tim Wright, *Tescape, Glasgow, UK*

Aboubakr Zade, *Middlesex University, London, UK*

Introduction to Leading Issues in Social Knowledge Management – A brief and personal history of Knowledge Management!

In its early days, Knowledge Management (KM) was primarily about capturing all the messy unstructured information in an organization; making it searchable and easily accessible to employees. It's still what most companies mean when they talk about KM - so much so, that many IT managers think this is all there is to KM.

KM in this techno-centric form grew up with the development of the Internet, organizational intranets and portals and the widespread use of electronic mail, Microsoft Office, corporate search engines and the like. It is fundamentally technology driven; usually by the IT department. It is centrally controlled and top-down in nature.

Techno-centric KM is necessary and useful but is not without its problems. Many early KM systems were designed to capture corporate information by requiring people to enter stuff into databases or to create personal profiles to help people find expertise. But too often employees did not see the value in this and such systems failed.

But meanwhile other organizations were starting to practise a form of KM that relied not on technology but on softer tools that enabled people to share information face to face - tools such as communities of practice, after action reviews, peer assists and knowledge cafes.

This people-centric form of KM evolved in parallel with the techno-centric variety and is more about informal learning, collaboration and inter-personal knowledge sharing. The objective is improved communication, better decision making, greater creativity and innovation where as techno-centric KM is more about efficiency – being able to quickly find the right information when you need it.

Quite separately, while all of this was taking place, social tools were start-ing to evolve on the web: blogs, wikis; social tagging and the like. These tools are very different to traditional corporate knowledge sharing tools. They were originally not developed by the large software developers such as Microsoft or IBM though that is changing. They are often open source and free or very low cost and they are built around open protocols.

Social tools put knowledge sharing power in the hands of the users them-selves – so much so that the term "user" is no longer really appropriate. And it's this, to a great degree that has accounted for their rapid evolution, uptake and success.

As these new tools took hold, people started to talk about Web 2.0. A new web dominated by social tools and the philosophy that they embedded, turning the web of Web 1.0 from a publishing medium to a two way com-munication and knowledge sharing medium – the so called "participatory web".

And now as these tools migrate into organizations people are talking about Enterprise 1.0 and Enterprise 2.0 (E2.0). Enterprise 1.0 is seen as a tradi-tional top down command and control, hierarchical organization built around traditional centralized IT systems while Enterprise 2.0 is a flatter, more fluid networked organization built around social tools.

It wasn't KM people who drove this development. It wasn't the traditional KM IT vendors and it wasn't the KM managers and workers within organi-zations. It was a bunch of enthusiastic renegades on the web as well as a few corporate renegades who could see where things were heading.

But KM managers, practitioners and others are starting to see the power of social tools within organizations as personal KM tools. And a new view is emerging of KM 2.0 that maps many of the principals of Web 2.0 and Enterprise 2.0 onto KM.

Clearly though, "2.0" stuff does not replace "1.0" stuff as the suffix might imply: traditional "1.0" thinking and tools run hand in hand with "2.0" stuff. Organizations need both and they are co-evolving.

But the key word in all of this is the word social. Another label for KM 2.0 is "Social KM". It is an emerging social model of KM. To my mind it is a very powerful model as it clearly places responsibility for knowledge sharing and making knowledge productive in the hands of the individual.

And so in the world of Social KM we have two categories of social tool – soft-tools such as after action reviews and knowledge cafes and techno-tools such as wikis and blogs – an incredibly powerful combination.

1   Making sense of Social Business

In the early days, Social Tools (blogs, wikis and the like) tended to be called Social Networking or Social Computing but as these tools entered the corporate realm, the dominant name became Social Media.

More recently, Social Tools have been adopted widely within organizations and called Enterprise 2.0 to set them apart from their use on the web and the realm of Web 2.0.

Then in 2007, I was one of the first to talk about Social KM – using Social Tools to help manage and share knowledge.

With so many terms, it is all a little confusing: Social Tools, Social Software, Social Computing, Social Networking, Social Media, Social Marketing, Social KM, Web 2.0 and Enterprise 2.0. To make matters worse, everyone has a different take on what they mean and their meaning is changing over time. To my mind though, this is OK, given the rapid evolution of the tools and their application.

More recently still, people have started to talk about Social Business. So what is Social Business?

Many people think Enterprise 2.0 is only about the technology while others think it is about the technology plus the organizational structures, processes and behaviours that govern their use.

To my mind, Enterprise 2.0 and Social Business are the same though I personally prefer Social Business as a term.

Others, who see Enterprise 2.0 as solely about technology, will probably continue to use both terms to draw a distinction, though I would rather see the E2.0 label dropped and replaced by the term Social Computing or Social Software.

So where does Social KM fit into all of this? Well if Social Business is the umbrella for the use of social tools within an organization then both Social Media and Social KM can be seen as part of Social Business.

In summary taking a simplistic, tools centred view:
- Social Computing or Social Software is the technology.
- Social Tools are both technology tools such as blogs and wikis and soft tools such as after action reviews and knowledge cafes.
- Social Marketing is about using Social Tools for a marketing purpose.
- Social Media is about using Social Tools for a marketing or communication purpose.
- Social Networking is about using Social tools to network.
- Social KM is about using Social Tools for a KM purpose such as knowledge sharing or collaboration.
- Social Business (aka Enterprise 2.0) is all of the above and more. It's about how social tools are used by a business in its totality.

This is a good start in understanding Social Business but we have to remember that although these have been the drivers, it is not so much about the tools or the technology - it's about a fundamental shift in how we work. It's about moving from hierarchies to networks; to a business world where knowledge sharing, collaboration, connectedness and relationships are important and are leveraged towards business objectives. Social Business is more a mindset and an approach to business than it is about technology.

But one final twist.

The term Social Business has an alternative meaning that has been around a little longer than in the Enterprise 2.0 sense.

A Social Business is a non-loss, non-dividend company designed to address a social objective. This use of the term has grown from the work of people: Muhammad Yunus and the Grameen Bank that he founded to provide micro-credit to the poor, would be a prime example of a Social Business. The measure of success of a social business is not profit but the impact that it has on society, on people and on the environment.

We need more social businesses to create a sustainable world. In order to survive, we need to collaborate more, to make better decisions and to be more innovative. This to me is what KM is about and is its future.

We need Social Business in both senses of the term.

2   The papers selected for this book

In selecting the papers for this book I have chosen ones that in some way research the use of Web 2.0 tools or technologies for knowledge sharing or informal learning within business organizations though one or two are more relevant to educational settings.

I must confess that quite naturally these papers tend to reflect my focus and personal views on Social KM but I hope this helps give some sense of coherence to the subject matter and to the book.

In my brief editorial commentaries I have tried to quite concisely describe the purpose of each paper and to extract one or two key insights that I see as important and to add some personal commentary of my own.

I have enjoyed reading the papers and contributing to the book and would like to congratulate the authors, many of whom I know personally, on some fine work.

Enjoy reading the book and let me leave you with one of my favorite quotes from Plutarch, the Greek historian.

"The mind is not a vessel to be filled, but a fire to be kindled."

David Gurteen
Gurteen Knowledge
Fleet, England
May 2012

Is the Emergence of Social Software a Source of Knowledge Management Revival?

Aurilla Aurelie Arntzen Bechina[1] and Vincent Ribiere[2]
[1]Buskerud University College, Kongsberg, Norway
[2]Bangkok University, Bangkok, Thailand
Originally published in the Proceedings of ECKM 2009

Editor's Commentary

This paper discusses the role of Social Media in what the authors see as a KM renaissance but that I see as a natural evolution of KM. They point out that in the past, many KM projects have not been successful and that one of the main reasons for this is the failure to take the people and organisational culture into account. They see Social Media as turning passive consumers of information into active participants. To me this is at the heart of what Social KM is all about. As the authors so rightly say in their conclusion, technological innovations are not magic bullets, and will not provoke organisational change by just being deployed.

Abstract: Lately, a debate regarding Knowledge Management decline has risen. Even though most of top executives recognize that knowledge is a strategic asset that leads to increase business performance, KM implementation remains problematic. The main barriers remain in its adoption by all types of users and contributors. Many companies reported examples of Knowledge Management initiatives that were not as successful as expected. Failures are often due to lack of employee's enthusiasm to participate actively in the Knowledge sharing processes or to the opacity of social relationships linking people across the organizations. The persistent quest to achieve KM objectives and to foster collaboration has led strategists to consider emerging technologies, such as social software, to support new networked and informal business structures. This paper discuses the role of social software in the knowledge management renaissance.

1

Keywords: Social software, Knowledge Management, knowledge sharing, Web2.0, technologies, organizational culture

1 Introduction

In the knowledge economy, challenges such as fierce competitions, globalisation, customer need's changes, and technology evolvement are driving companies to set up strategies to manage their intellectual assets (Kuhlen, 2003). Knowledge management has emerged from different disciplines and technological trends encompassing for examples learning theories, competences management, Software engineering, organisational behaviour and Business management. Knowledge Management (KM) is considered as a crucial strategy contributing to improve the competiveness and performance of companies (Argote, McEvily, & Reagans, 2003). Numerous research works and case studies have demonstrated the benefits of KM in leveraging corporate knowledge and fostering innovation within the organisations (Abdullah, 2005; T. H. Davenport, De Long, & Beers, 1998; Dixon, 2002; Gupta & Michailova, 2004). Although, companies recognise the vital importance of managing corporate, they are still ongoing debates on the real business value of knowledge management. While some organisations report some tangible outcomes from KM implementations, others do not see any substantial benefits.

The main reported issues are often related to the lack of adoption by the employees of knowledge management systems (KMS). Poor contributions to the KMS have been often reported (Fu & Lee, 2005; Gee-Woo, Robert W. Zmud, Young-Gul, & Jae-Nam, 2005). The reasons are multiple and include poor user interface or navigation design, complex, pour search functionality and so forth (Abdullah, 2005).

Failures are as well attributed to the lack of employee's enthusiasm to participate actively in the Knowledge sharing processes or even to the opacity of social relationships linking people across the organizations (Ardichvili, Page, & Wentling, 2003; Hoogenboom., Kloos., Bouman., & Jansen., 2007). The persistent quest to achieve KM objectives and to foster collaboration has led strategists to consider emerging technologies, such as social software, to support new networked and informal business structures(Adamides & Karacapilidis, 2006; Peter Burkhardt, 2009).

This paper outlines the role of social software in the knowledge management renaissance. The current technologies are presented and Web2.0 concepts contributing to the renewal of Knowledge Management is presented.

2 Knowledge/knowledge managements technologies

2.1 Background

Due to the current changing business environment, organisations are facing challenges of global competitiveness. The quest for competitiveness and sustainability has led to recognition of the efficient use of information and communication technologies as a vital ingredient for survival and profitability in the knowledge-based economy. Knowledge is seen by many as a key source of competitive advantage and innovation in organisations.

Knowledge is defined as information in context and it is necessary to recognize the different types of knowledge in order to expose its potential contribution to the performance of the organization (Pemberton & Stonehouse, 2000). The wide-based knowledge definitions highlight the presence of several forms of knowledge; tacit, explicit, implicit and systemic knowledge at the individual, group and organisational levels (T. Davenport & Prusak, 2000; Dixon, 2002; Inkpen, 1996; Nonaka & Takeuchi, 1995; Polanyi, 1958).

Explicit knowledge has a tangible dimension that can be easily captured, codified and communicated (Firestone, 2001). In contrast, tacit knowledge is linked to intuition, emotions, beliefs, know-how, experiences and values. The distinction between tacit and explicit knowledge is important since their management is quite distinctive and requires different knowledge management initiatives and technologies deployment. Traditionally, depending of the type of knowledge, companies would adopt a codification or personalisation strategy.

Codification tools and practices intend to collect, codify, and disseminate knowledge artefacts. One of the benefits of the codification approach is the reuse of knowledge. The aim of codification is to put organizational knowledge into a form that makes it accessible to those who need it (T. H. Davenport, et al., 1998). Knowledge is codified using a **people-to-documents approach**: it is extracted from the person who developed it,

3

made independent of that person, and reused for various purposes" (M. Hansen, N. Nohria, & T. Tierney, 1999).

Personalization tools and practices focus on developing networks for linking people so that tacit knowledge can be shared or transferred. The personalisation strategy relies on person-to-person contact for sharing knowledge and experiences. The corporate memory is based on its individuals, and information technology is used primarily as a means to locate knowledgeable
people and enable direct communication (M. Hansen, et al., 1999). Information and Communication Technologies (ICT) are moderately used in such type of approach.

What is the best strategy between personalization and codification? Hansen et al. (1999) noted that effective organizations excel by primarily emphasizing one of the approaches and using the other in a supporting role. They postulate that companies trying to excel at both approach risk failing at both. They refer to a 20-80 split between codification and personalization. This proposal raised much discussion in the literature (Koenig & Kanti Srikantaiah, 2004). After conducting a survey among 100 US companies involved in KM, Ribière (2005b) showed that the companies studied were more likely to use a balanced approach with a ratio closer from 45%-55% than from 20%-80%, as suggested by Hansen et al (1999).

Thus, Knowledge management (KM) initiatives are various and are expanding across all types of organizations and companies worldwide (Ribière, Bechina Arntzen, & Worasinchai, 2007). The KM project implementation can be very different; it ranges from building knowledge based repositories to social software deployment. Several documented benefits resulting from the successful implementation of KM have been published (Alavi & Leidner, 2001; Becerra-Fernandez, Gonzalez, & Sabherwal, 2004; Coleman, 1998; Jennex & Olfman, 2004).

The earlier KM implementations focused strongly on the Information Communication Technology (ICT); however most of the researchers and practitioners recognise the importance of the "soft" dimensions of KM initiatives (Anantatmula, 2005; Gee-Woo, et al., 2005; Ribière, 2005a). Thus the social aspects of ICT are more and more taken in account while deploying a KM implementation.

4

Today, plethora of available tools, technologies and approaches are contributing to increase the confusion in how to implement the best suited KM initiatives for the company's' needs (Murray & Peyrefitte, 2007).

Therefore, a general technological framework that will guide a KM implementation is needed. In the next section, based on literature reviews, we outline a Knowledge type driven framework of KM technologies.

2.2 A Knowledge type driven framework of KM technologies

This following framework illustrates the different KM technologies based on the type of information and Knowledge artefacts (KAs) they manage (Figure 1). The bottom part (factory building) represents the corporate data, information and knowledge artefacts; The top part is linked to the Internet (cloud) and to the different stakeholders and environment factors.

The left part of the figure represents tacit KAs and the right part explicit KAs that can be broken down into structured and unstructured information. The two parts overlap since most knowledge is neither fully tacit nor explicit.

Each of the following sections refers to the parts of figure1.

Section ❶ represents tools used to manage structured information (i.e., records); examples include database management systems.

Section ❷ represents tools that can be used to support both structured and unstructured information. These tools can be applied to search and manipulate information in database repositories but also in documents. For instance a semantic engine might be used to extract the key concepts out of a document and to display them on a map or on a tag cloud (e.g., visualization tool).

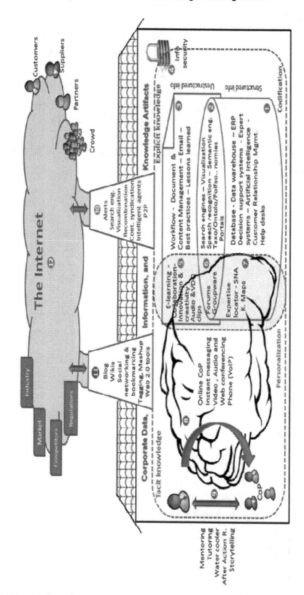

Figure 1: KM technologies framework (Ribière, 2009b)

As previously mentioned, since KAs represent a large proportion of the intellectual asset of an organization they need to be properly protected (section❹). Information Security tools and practices need to be implemented to secure and to protect information. Over protecting information might impact the ability of employees to fully take advantage of the corporate knowledge asset, and leaving everyone access to everything might also result in knowledge leaks that might affect the company's competitiveness. Therefore, it is crucial for the organisation to balance both requirements.

Section ❺ describes the tools that can support unstructured information (i.e., explicit KAs) and tacit KAs. If we refer to Nonaka's and Takeushi's SECI model (1995), these tools could support both the Codification (i.e., conversion from tacit to explicit) and the Internalization (i.e., conversion from explicit to tacit) phases. Creativity and Innovation support tools as well as collaborative tools can facilitate the emergence of new ideas by supporting and stimulating interactions between groups. Audio and video recordings of expert interviews and any type of debriefing sessions can be valuable if they are, later on, properly converted into short video clips associated with meaningful keywords/tags that will make them easily retrievable. E-learning tools support the learning process and the creation of tacit knowledge through practice and errors.

Section ❻ describes the tools that can support explicit KAs (based on both structured and unstructured information) as well as tacit KAs. Groupware application and online forums facilitate the capture and exchange of various types of information and documents. Database Management systems are used to link/connect these various types of information that makes them easier to manage and which also provide a context for their understanding.

Section ❼ describes the tools that can support structured information (i.e., explicit KAs) and tacit KAs. Expertise locators (also called corporate yellow pages, or who is who) can be used to identify who in the organization has some particular expertise, skills, or knowledge about a specific topic. They help people to connect with each others. Knowledge maps can be used to identify where knowledge can be found and its flows. Social Network Analysis (SNA) allows you to identify the informal connection in between people inside and outside an organization. They can be used to identify who are the key holders of knowledge, who are knowledge brokers, hubs, etc.

Section ❽ describes the tools that can support the transfer/flow or tacit knowledge between individuals. Online Communities of Pratcice CoPs often provide the capabilities for members to have interactions through instant messaging, video-audio-Web conferencing, or through phone conversations (e.g., Voice over IP).

Section ❾ is not supported by technology but we represented it in order to reinforce the fact that tacit knowledge is best transferred by face to face interactions and socialization activities (e.g., mentoring, tutoring, water cooler discussions, after action reviews (AAR), and storytelling).

Section ❿ described the tools that can be used to search, visualize, and automatically retrieve (i.e., push technologies) information located on the Internet. These tools are critical to increase awareness about any new available information regarding your stakeholders or your environment represented on the Internet cloud ⓬ .

Finally, section ⓫ represents the new generation of Web 2.0 tools which facilitate people to share and connect with each other inside and outside the organization. The next section describes these Web 2.0 tools in more detail.

3   Social software and KM

3.1   The Web2.0 approach

Despite the fact that many current implementations of KM initiatives are based on highly advanced information technologies, there are still challenges to cope with in order to ensure the effectiveness and efficiency of such KM initiatives. Several studies and surveys having investigated the reasons leading to the KM initiative failure, highlighted that organizational culture and others psycho-social factors play an important role to the KM success (E&Y, 1996; Knowledge Management Review, 2001; Tuggle & Shaw, 2000).

Thus, with the growing recognition that KM technologies have not fully delivered their promises, academic and KM practitioners have shifted their focus on solving "non technological issues" related to practices, cultures, and organizational changes(Boulos & Wheeler, 2007). Knowledge sharing is seen as a challenging task, difficult to nurture within an organization. It requires pro-social behaviour through social processes, for example by cultivating a sense of community (Allen, 2008; Tapscott, 2006)

The persistent quest to achieve KM objectives and to foster collaboration has led strategist's people to adopt emerging technologies supporting new networked business structures. Web 2.0, Social software, could become one of the answers for improving the way people work together and to address some of the knowledge sharing challenges.

Close studies, looking at the use of Web 2.0 communities, show that knowledge sharing is the fundamental nature of such approaches. For example, strong user's participations have created the recognized success of some Web sites such as Wikipedia Ebay or Amazon.

With expanding capability to connect people and the need to enable corporate knowledge sharing, it is important to take a Swiss Army knife approach providing many tools and selecting the right tool or approach for each need at the point of use (Carla O'Dell, 2008). Therefore, it is crucial to understand the Web 2.0 concept, how a new breed of open, networked organization—the Enterprise 2.0 is emerging and why nowadays the KM practitioners are showing interests to the concept of Web2.0 and social software and the underlying promise of a better knowledge sharing support (Tapscott, 2006).

The Web 2.0 phenomenon has gained tremendous visibility and has attracted strong interests not only from the scientific community but as well from businesses and IT vendors (Smith, 2008). This has generated some conflicting definitions of Web 2.0 since IT vendors are trying to capitalize on this trend by associating their products with Web 2.0 attributes, like they did with KM technologies in the mid 90's.

Web 2.0 should be seen as the convergence of two driving trends, one technological oriented and one emphasizing social dimensions. This convergence leads to new business models with user-contributed content. The features leverage a diverse participatory intellectual capital to enhance the transparency of business processes and to distribute participatory services and products design.

The Web 2.0 definition by Tim O'Really, who first used this word, better reflects this new concept of gravitational core identified as the web as platform, user controlled data, architectures of participation, cost-effective scalability, re-mixable data source and data transmissions, and harnessing collective intelligence (Tapscott, 2006).

In opposition to Web 1.0, users can easily generate and publish content. The collective intelligence of users encourages more democratic use and participation (Boulos & Wheeler, 2007). Initially, the primarily goal of the World Wide Web (WWW) was to foster a better collaboration among the scientific communities by sharing ideas and knowledge. However, it is only with the emergence of Web 2.0 technologies that we start to recognize its impacts on leveraging knowledge sharing and enhancing business processes in organizations.

Web 2.0 is a platform for interacting with content. Information is broken up into "micro-content" units that may be distributed across the Web. A new set of tools such as RSS (Really Simple Syndication) provide mechanisms that creates a "feed" of updates from specified news sites, blogs and so forth. RSS contributes to publishing, aggregating and combining micro-content in new and useful ways.

3.2   Social software tools

Literature reviews indicate that the main focus of Web 2.0 is oriented toward the social networking dimensions of Web 2.0. It fosters the KM leitmotiv meaning from content collection to people connection. There is so far no common definition of the social software; however, there is a general consensus to recognize the strong interactive processes and networks as the backbone of such software. The interaction is mainly due to the shift from push driven to pull driven information, in which user-generated content is prevailing (Hoogenboom., et al., 2007; Johnston, 2007).

Social software applications and services are perceived as the outcome of the popularity and the rapid development of Web 2.0 concepts. Web 2.0

services are: wiki's, like Wikipedia; blogging, such as Blogger; social networking such as Facebook; and social bookmarking, such as Del.Icio.Us.

Wiki comes from the Hawaiian word for fast. Wiki is a collaborative mechanism that allows people to contribute or modify content using a simplified markup language. Wiki is usually used to support the community building website. Wikipedia, an open content encyclopedia, is considered as one of the most popular examples of a wikis. Wikis allow users to enter, aggregate, and annotate content. The underlying concept lies on the collective wisdom to produce an organized, thorough, and searchable database in various domains such as political, humanitarian, education, history, and so forth. However, There are some issues related to security and the content quality that need to be tackled without loosing the sight of the concept of free contribution (Peter Burkhardt, 2009).

Blogs are the most personal and controversial of the Web 2.0 applications and more especially in business contexts. Web sites can be created spontaneously and maintained by individuals making it possible to maintain an online journal on which others can comment for private use or business purpose. Hence, activities discussions can emerge from dynamic use of the Blogging feature. The biggest advantage resides in the possibility for participants to interact with others. For example, HP is encouraging its employee to use blog feature to discuss issues on printer compatibility with customers. Blogs have experienced exponential growth by enabling mass communication without requiring HTML knowledge; for example in 10 years the blog sites number has increased to more than 200 million (Raskino, 2007). However, it is important to notice there is need to understand further the knowledge sharing process in this setting. Several authors publish their own blog and if there are neither readers nor active participants, the interest of using a blog is quite limited.

Social networking is the practice of increasing the number of business or personal contact by making connections through individuals. This system allows members of a specific site to learn about other members' skills, talents, knowledge, or preferences regardless of geographic location. The concept of social networking is of course not new, however, the Internet has provided a strong potential to extend this phenomenon beyond the usual connections through a Web-based community. Popular Web sites dedicated to social networking include Myspace, Hi5, and Facebook. Professional examples dedicated to social networks include LinkedIn, XING, and Viadeo. These later sites are said to create business opportunities by enhancing communication among employees, customers who can learn about each other's background such as undertaken contact information, education, employment history, employment opportunities, and so forth (Tonellato, 2008).

Social bookmarking allows users to manage, store, organize, and search bookmarks of web pages. The bookmarks can be public, private, or shared only with a specific people or a given community, or the public. Social bookmark services allow users to organize their bookmarks online with informal tags instead of the traditional browser-based system of folders. Therefore, authorized people can view these bookmarks chronologically, by category or tags, or via a search engine. An interesting additional feature relies on the possibility to comment online, annotate or rate on bookmarks. Some social book markings provide web feeds allowing subscribers to become aware of creation, tagging, and saving of new bookmarks by other users. Examples include Flickrs and Delicious.

There are many available tools; however, it is important to understand the need of the users Web 2.0 and their limitations.

3.3   Who are the users of Web 2.0?

There is strong recognition that people responsible of implementing KM initiative also called KM practitioners are early adopters of knowledge related technologies. Hence, the novel Web 2.0 tools having social computing features were used easily by the KM practitioners. Usually, they are always looking for better tools and practices for the KM initiatives implemented in their workplaces. Examples include the large use of Wiki or Blogging (Redmiles & Wilensky, 2008).

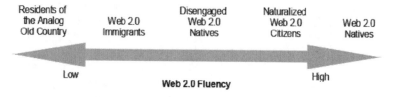

Figure 2: Spectrum of Web 2.0 fluency (Phifer, 2008)

However, with the expansion of Web 2.0 technologies, the concepts of Digital Natives and Digital Immigrants have emerged. Digital Natives are individuals who were born and grew up during the era of the Web, in which instant online access, instant communication with multiple peer groups are part of their thinking mode. Digital Immigrants were born and grew up before this era. Individuals belong either to Digital Native or to Digital Immigrant groups. Digital native have a more intuitive potential than digital immigrant to adopt quickly what Web 2.0 offers (Phifer, 2008). However, motivation of using Web 2.0 technologies is the decisive element.

For a successful deployment and use of Web 2.0 technologies, it is crucial to categorize the Web 2.0 users in order for enterprises to understand how to deal with employees, customers. Psychographics are essential, because they relate to the user's lifestyle, interests, aspirations and attitudes towards the use of tool such blogs, wiki, and social networks. It is not the age of the person that determines the categories but rather the people inclination to use Web 2.0 technologies.

One manifestation and application of Web 2.0 in the business domain refers to the concept of Enterprise 2.0 and that has greatly contributed to the renewal of Knowledge Management.

3.4 Enterprise 2.0: A new way to do business

During the last decade, enterprise strategists started to recognize that business success and performance improvement was more and more related to the degree to which it is a knowledge based organization. There is no doubt that sharing knowledge culture, building a strong sense of community, collaborating, and networking people can drastically contribute to the business process improvement and give to the organization a competitive advantage. Based on collaboration and cooperation, the renaissance of KM and its underlying concepts is leading to a new concept of Enterprise 2.0 (Gotta, 2007).

The term "Enterprise 2.0", E2.0 describes a collection of organizational and IT practices that help organizations establish flexible work models, visible knowledge-sharing practices, and higher levels of community participation. An additional interesting feature of E2.0 is the "mashup" - a website or web application that uses content from more than one source to create a completely new service.

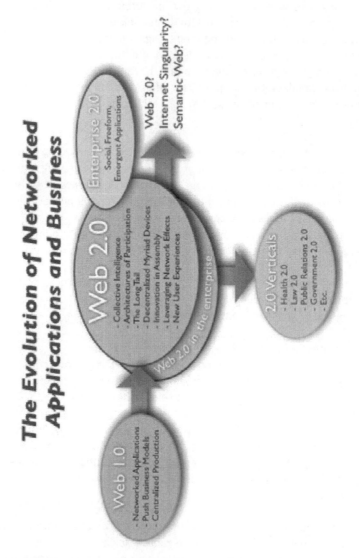

Figure 3: Evolution of networked enterprises (Hinchcliffe, 2008)

E2.0 refers to the use of social software in order to improve knowledge sharing and foster collaboration between companies, employees, theirs customers, and partners. To illustrate this approach, Tascop (2006) introduce "the term of wikinomics to describe an economy in which companies are gaining competitive advantage by successfully managing a trust-based relationships with external collaborators and customers" (Johnston, 2007; Tapscott, 2006). The last decade has seen a clear evolution toward a networked enterprises concept as a means for companies to be more competitive. Figure 3 illustrates the evolution from Web 1.0 to Enterprise 2.0.

The growing adoption of E2.0 is dictated by the need to capitalize knowledge and to retain the corporate knowledge assets through a well thought human resource strategies and competence based management. In addition, the pressure on firms to innovate has forced firms to look for ways to improve their business performances. E2.0 represents a new paradigm for strategic collaboration and KM.

There is no doubt that KM initiatives coupled with collaboration efforts are the best strategy to address the needs to retain people and reach performance goals. Although Enterprise 2.0 seems to bring the right answer, it is necessary to examine what constitutes the framework of E 2.0.

McAfee (2006) introduced the terms and concepts behind E2.0. He has coined mnemonic **SLATES** to describe the key aspects of these social platforms with a description of the essential elements. **SLATES** stands for Search, Links, Authorship, Tags, Extensions, and Signals.

- *Search technologies* should allow the discovery of the E2.0 content. So that it can be reused or leveraged. This is an important feature that will enhance the collaboration aspects by incorporating this function into business processes.

- *Links* denotes the possibility to integrate content such as Mashup (i.e., re-mixing the contents in other to create a new one) by facilitating the interconnections between content. It facilitates as well the navigation through the content.

- *Authorship* refers to the usability of the system by allowing access to every worker without having to enter into an extensive training program.

- *Tags* allow the use of meta-tags in order to identify the relevancy of tagged content. Tags create a taxonomy, or several taxonomies, and can be combined to create a Folksonomy. Tags can be used to capture individual and collective opinions on the value of content, a form of knowledge in itself, which can also be used as a navigational path through content in a manner similar to links.

- *Extensions* introduce technology to expose patterns of user activity in order to get an insight from the knowledge base. Mechanisms for searching user activity and its behaviour are as well provided such for instance Users who have searched on this topic, have also looked at this.

- *Signal* refers to the use of specific technology to push content to potential interested users. It gives a proactively collaborative feature to E2.0. For example, users can subscribe to a Web site and get immediately informed if any changes occurred in meantime.

3.5   Limitations and barriers

It is recognized among the KM Practitioners that focusing only on technologies will not insure the success of Web 2.0 deployment. E2.0 could have happen even without technologies due to the fact that it is a socially-driven evolution that did not originate from a technology push nor from a demand pull (AAIM, 2008). Hence, adopting E2.0 is not about using others software tools but rather means that people have to reconsider their business routine by incorporating the collaborative paradigm in their daily work. Organizational dimension should be considered by fostering change management strategy while trying to implement new technology. Understanding organizational challenges means understanding the E2.0 adoption barriers, which identify the critical success factors (Gotta, 2007).

The penetration of new technologies in the workplace has generated new type of issues and challenges. For example, selection and adoption of technology is a complex process that is based on a number of alternatives including technological choices, perceived benefits, cost based models and organizational strategies. However technology itself needs adaptation to organizational goals and strategies (Laulmann, Nadler, and O'Farrell, 1991).

Motivations for technology use are both intrinsic and extrinsic. Adaptability of technology to user needs, user confidence, and motivation to its adoption are key factors to undertand. Kanter's has identified five charac-teristics of successful technology adoption, the five Fs -: **F**ocused, **F**ast, **F**lexible, **F**riendly, and **F**un (Kanter, 1990).

The deployment of novel Web 2.0 tools requires understanding the factors that will facilitate or inhibit the full adoption of their use in the workplace. It is important to examine some of the organizational issues that E2.0 must face such as governance, culture, leadership, incentive schemes, and value capture.

One factor related to the organizational culture arises from the fact that some organizations do not promote extensive collaboration and knowl-edge sharing outside their project teams. Thus, the Web 2.0 deployment is a challenging task.

Another factor common in many industries (e.g., manufacturing's, aero-space, automation) is the generation gap. Workforces in these sectors are aging and belong mainly to the digital immigrant group. Hence, it is chal-lenging for some of them to use or see a need for social software in their daily work.

4 Conclusion

It is commonly agreed that although there are plenty of technical solutions supporting different knowledge processes such as knowledge creation, representation, storage, and sharing and so forth, there is still a need to understand the factors impacting not only the acceptance of the knowl-edge management systems (KMS) by the knowledge worker but also their efficient usage. Studies and surveys having investigated the reasons lead-ing to the KM initiative failure, highlighted that organizational culture and others psycho-social factors play an important role to the KM success. Therefore, the penetration of social aspects into the development and use of information communication platform have contributed to gain further interests into Knowledge management processes.

During the past few years, there has been a growing interest in social soft-ware under the name of Web2.0 for both the business world and the aca-demic communities. Web2.0 represents the revolution that is happening since more and more users are transforming from passive consumers status to active participants. Today the tasks independency that workers have to perform requires a flow of information and a high level of knowledge sharing and thanks to the emergence of Web2.0, this is today a reality that is happening.

However, technological innovations are not magic bullets, and will not provoke organizational change by just being deployed. Enterprise 2.0 technologies must be introduced into a dynamic environment that participants can see value in. This can be done by taking into accounts human and social contexts and providing appropriate management visioning of the future.

References

Abdullah, R., Selamat Mohd Hasan, Sahibudin, Shamsul and Alinda Alias Rose (2005). A Framework For Knowledge Management System Implementation In Collaborative Environment For Higher Learning Institution. *Journal of Knowledge Management Practice*.

Adamides, E. D., & Karacapilidis, N. (2006). Information technology support for the knowledge and social processes of innovation management. *Technovation, 26*(1), 50-59.

Alavi, M., & Leidner, D. E. (2001). Review: Knowledge Management and Knowledge Management Systems: Conceptual Foundations and Research Issues. *MIS Quarterly, 25*, 107-136.

Allen, P. J. (2008, 26-28 June 2008). *How Web 2.0 communities solve the knowledge sharing problem.* Paper presented at the Technology and Society, IEEE International Symposium , ISTAS Fredericton, New Brunswick, Canada.

Anantatmula, V. (2005). Outcomes of Knowledge Management Initiatives. *International Journal of Knowledge Management, 1*(2), 50-67.

Ardichvili, A., Page, V., & Wentling, T. (2003). Motivation and barriers to participation in virtual knowledge-sharing communities of practice. *Journal of Knowledge Management, 7*(1), 76-78.

Argote, L., McEvily, B., & Reagans, R. (2003). Managing knowledge in organisations: An integrative framework and review of emerging themes. *Management Science, 49*(4), 571-582.

Becerra-Fernandez, I., Gonzalez, A., & Sabherwal (2004). *Knowledge management: challenges, solutions and technologies*. Upper Saddle River, NJ: Pearson Education, Inc.

Boulos, K. M., N. , & Wheeler, S. (2007). The emerging Web 2.0 social software: an enabling suite of sociable technologies in health and health care education. *Health Information and Libraries Journal, 24, 24*, pp 2-23.

Carla O'Dell (2008). *Web 2.0 and Knowledge Management.*

Chua, A., & Lam, W. (2005). Why KM projects fail: a multi-case analysis. *Journal of Knowledge Management, 9*(3), 6-17.

Coleman, V. (1998). *Knowledge Management at Chase Manhattan Bank.* Paper presented at the Knowledge Management: A New Frontier in Human Resources?

Davenport, T., & Prusak, L. (2000). Working Knowledge. *Harvard Business School Press.*

Davenport, T. H., De Long, D. W., & Beers, M. (1998). Successful Knowledge Management Projects. *Sloan Management Review*, 43-57.

Dixon, N. (2002). Common knowledge: How companies thrive by sharing what they know. *Boston: Harvard Business Press.*

E&Y (1996). *KM International Survey*: Ernst & Young.

Firestone, J. M. (2001). Key issues in knowledge management. journal of knowledge management consortium international, 1(3). *Knowledge and Innovation: Journal of the KMCI, 1*(3).

Fu, S., & Lee, M. (2005). *IT-Based Knowledge Sharing and Organizational Trust: The Development and Initial Test of a Comprehensive Model,.* Paper presented at the European Conference on Information Systems.

Gee-Woo, B., Robert W. Zmud, Young-Gul, K., & Jae-Nam, L. (2005). Behavioral Intention Formation Knowledge Sharing: Examining Roles Of Extrinsic Motivators, Social-Psychological Forces, and Organizational Climate. *MIS Quarterly, 29*(1).

Gotta, M. (2007). *Enterprise 2.0: Collaboration and Knowledge Management Renaissance.* Midvale, Utah.

Gupta, K., & Michailova, S. (2004). Knowledge Sharing in Knowledge-Intensive Firms: Opportunities and Limitations of Knowledge Codification, . *CKG WP* Retrieved from http://frontpage.cbs.dk/ckg/upload/CKG-WP%202004-12.pdf

Hansen, M., Nohria, N., & Tierney, T. (1999). What's your strategy for managing knowledge? *Harvard Business Review 7*(2), 106-116.

Hansen, M. T., Nohria, N., & Tierney, T. (1999). What's your strategy for managing knowledge? *Harvard Business Review, 77*(2), 106-116.

Hinchcliffe, D. (2008, February, 26). Dion Hinchcliffe's Web 2.0 Blog. http://web2.socialcomputingmagazine.com/web20_continues_as_most_u sed_new_internet_term.htm.

Hoogenboom., T., Kloos., M., Bouman., W., & Jansen., R. (2007). Sociality and learning in social software. *International Journal of Knowledge and Learning, 3*(4-5), Pages 501-514.

Inkpen, A. (1996). Creating knowledge through collaboration. *California Management Review, 39*(1), 123 -140.

Jennex, M. E., & Olfman, L. (2004). *Assessing Knowledge Management Success/Effectiveness Models.* Paper presented at the 37th Hawaii International Conference on System Sciences.

Johnston, K. (2007). Folksonomies, Collaborative Filtering and e-Business: is Enterprise 2.0 One Step Forward and Two Steps Back? *5*(4), 411-418

Kaweevisultrakul, T., & Chan, P. (2007). Impact of cultural barriers on Knowledge Manageement Implementation: Evidence from Thailand. *Journal of American Academy of Business, 11*(1), 303-309.

Knowledge Management Review (2001, November/December). KM Review survey reveals the challenges faced by practitioners, *4,* 8-9.

Koenig, M. E. D., & Kanti Srikantaiah, T. (2004). Knowledge Management Lessons Learned: What Works and What Doesn't, Information Today. *American Society for Information Science and Technology, Silver Spring, MD, Monograph Series,* 87-112

Kuhlen, R. (2003). *Change of Paradigm in Knowledge Management. Framework for the collaborative production and exhange of knowledge.* Paper presented at the World Library and Information Congress: 69 IFLA General Conference and Council, Berlin.

McAfee, A. (2006). Enterprise 2.0: The Dawn of Emergent Collaboration. *MIT Sloan Management Review, 47*(3), 21-28.

Murray, S., & Peyrefitte, J. (2007). Knowledge Type and Communication Media Choice in the Knowledge Transfer Process. *Journal of Managerial, XIX*(1).

Nonaka, I., & Takeuchi, H. (1995). The Knowledge-Creating Company. *Oxford University Press.*

Pemberton, J. D., & Stonehouse, G. H. (2000). Organizational learning and knowledge assets – an essential partnership. *The Learning Organization, 7*(4), pp 184-193.

Peter Burkhardt (2009). Social Software Trends in Business:. Retrieved from http://www.igi-global.com/downloads/excerpts/8352.pdf

Phifer, G. (2008). Web 2.0 User Categories: Beyond Digital Natives and Digital Immigrants. *ID Number: G00164326.* Retrieved from http://www.gartner.com/AnalystBiography?authorId=10250

Polanyi, M. (1958). *Personal knowledge*: Chicago University Press.

Raskino, M. (2007). *Enterprise Web 2.0 Goes Mainstream* (No. Gartner G00153218).

Redmiles, D., & Wilensky, H. (2008). *Adoption of Web 2.0 in the Enterprise: Technological Frames of KM Practitioners and Users.* Paper presented at the Workshop for CSCW 2008. from http://swiki.cs.colorado.edu:3232/CSCW2008-Web20/33

Ribière, V. (2005a). Building a Knowledge-Centered Culture: a Matter of Trust. In M. A. Stankosky (Ed.), *Creating the Discipline of Knowledge Management*: Elsevier / Butterworth-Heinemann.

Ribière, V. (2005b). *Le rôle primordial de la confiance dans les démarches de gestion du savoir.* Unpublished PhD dissertation (Management Sciences) Université Paul Cézanne, Aix en Provence (France) - available on Proquest.

Ribière, V., Bechina Arntzen, A., A., & Worasinchai, L. (2007, November 21-23, 2007). *The Influence of Trust on the Success of Codification and Personalization KM Approaches.* Paper presented at the 5th International Conference on ICT and Higher Education, Bangkok, Thailand.

Smith, D. M. (2008). Web 2.0 and Beyond: Evolving the Discussion. *Gartner, Number: G00154767.* Retrieved from http://mslibrary/research/MktResearch/Gartner2/research/154700/154767/154767.html

Tapscott, D. (2006). Winning with the Enterprise 2.0. Retrieved from http://www.cob.sjsu.edu/jerrell_l/Tapscott%20on%20Collab%20Advantage.pdf

Tonellato, M. (2008). *Enterprise 2.0: Freeform, Social, Emergent Platforms for Collaboration and Knowledge Sharing. The case of Intesa SanPaolo.*, University of Lugano.

Tuggle, F. D., & Shaw, N. C. (2000, May). *The effect of organizational culture on the implementation of knowledge management.* Paper presented at the Florida Artificial Intelligence Research Symposium (FLAIRS), Orlando, FL.

AAIM (2008). Enterprise 2.0: Agile, Emergent & Integrated. *MarketIQ . Intelligence Quarterly.*

Exploring Web 2.0 Applications as a Means of Bolstering up Knowledge Management

Thomas Bebensee, Remko Helms, Marco Spruit
Utrecht University, Department of Information and Computing Sciences, Utrecht, Netherlands
Originally published in the Proceedings of ECKM 2010

> **Editorial Commentary**
> By conducting exploratory case studies in two organizations this research paper examines how Web 2.0 applications can be used for managing knowledge and what impact they have on KM. Based on their research, the authors speculate that the use of these applications may lead to a novel form of KM that is based on active user contributions and unbounded collaboration. I agree but to my mind it is not so much a novel form of KM but a natural evolution of KM. It is the essence of Social KM.

Abstract: Web 2.0 applications aim at improving the interaction between users. Web 2.0 principles overlap with characteristics of knowledge management (KM) or could be applied to reshape KM practices. Applying Web 2.0 applications to KM has the potential to improve the sharing and creation of knowledge. However, little research has been conducted in this area. This research aims at identifying Web 2.0 applications for bolstering up organizations' KM practices. An additional aspect addressed is how Web 2.0 applications for KM can be categorized and how they match different aspects of the KM strategy of an organization.

The research examines the suitability of Web 2.0 applications in KM by conducting exploratory case studies in two student-run organizations, which are an interesting research subject because their members are considered most open towards new technologies. The case studies aim at exploring which Web 2.0 applications are in place. Based on the findings we propose a framework for categorizing Web 2.0 applications for KM.

The findings indicate that Web 2.0 applications may enhance KM and may even initiate a new era of KM. Moreover, the article provides a discussion of a number of Web 2.0 applications and proposes a way of categorizing these applications. The proposed framework allows assessing the use of Web 2.0 applications for KM and can be used as an orientation for the introduction of Web 2.0 applications in organizational KM.

The research contributes to the general understanding of how Web 2.0 applications can be used in KM. The proposed framework for categorizing Web 2.0 applications provides an orientation for organizations that want to use these applications for bolstering up their KM practices.

Keywords: Web 2.0, Collective Intelligence, User-Generated Content, Social Computing, Knowledge Management, KM 2.0

1 Introduction

Today, an increasing amount of organizations recognize the importance of their workforces' knowledge as assets leveraging competitive advantage. This development gave rise to the emergence of knowledge management (KM). The KM discipline describes how knowledge-intensive organizations can develop a strategy and design an approach to manage the creation, sharing and application of knowledge in order to perform better and reach their overall strategic goals (Dalkir 2005).

With the dot-com crash in 2001, a new era of the World Wide Web began, which is often referred to as Web 2.0 (O'Reilly 2007). Since then organizations have begun to adopt Web 2.0 applications and techniques such as wikis and social networking for leveraging and improving their core processes (Chui et al. 2009). A systematic search on Google Scholar and other literature databases with different combinations of the keywords "Web 2.0" and "knowledge management" and some of their synonyms revealed that little research has been conducted to examine the impact of Web 2.0 on organizational KM practices. This brings us to our research question:

How can organizations use Web 2.0 applications for managing knowledge and which impact do they have on KM?

By conducting explorative case studies the research contributes to the general understanding of how Web 2.0 applications can be used to support or enable KM. The results are captured in a framework of Web 2.0 applications that organizations can use for bolstering up their KM practices.

The paper is structured as follows. Section 2 gives an introduction to the field of KM and Web 2.0. Section 3 presents the findings from the case studies. Section discusses the findings and a KM spectrum for Web 2.0 applications is proposed. Section 5 contains conclusions and indicates areas of further research.

2 Theoretical background

This section elaborates on relevant aspects of KM, Web 2.0 and the implication of Web 2.0 on organizations.

2.1 Knowledge management

KM is a young but relevant field in today's economy. Jashapara defines it as "the effective learning process associated with exploring, exploitation and sharing of human knowledge that use the appropriate technology and cultural environments to enhance an organization's intellectual capital and performance" (Jashapara 2004). In many large organizations, knowledge-management projects have been run, resulting in overall success (Davenport et al. 1999).

However, KM encompasses a variety of different aspects and can be regarded from a number of perspectives. Binney's (2001) KM Spectrum combines various KM theories, tools and techniques discussed in literature in one single framework. The six elements of the KM spectrum are:

- *Transactional KM applications* present knowledge to the user in the course of an interaction with a system.
- *Analytical KM solutions* allow for creating new knowledge from vast amounts of data or information by providing certain interpretations.

- *Asset management* involves the managing of knowledge assets and making them available to people when they are needed.
- *Process-Based KM* deals with the codification and improvement of processes in order to come up with 'engineered assets'. This often involves using methodologies stemming from other disciplines such as Total Quality Management.
- *Developmental KM* aims at improving and developing the competencies or capabilities of an organization's knowledge workers including both tacit and explicit knowledge.
- *Innovation and creation KM* fosters an environment in which knowledge workers, preferably with different backgrounds, can come together to create new knowledge.

In the following we use Binney's framework for analyzing KM in two organizations.

2.2   Web 2.0

A glance at Google's search history shows an increasing interest for the term "Web 2.0" since its emergence in the early 2000s. This shows the term's popularity but what does it actually stand for? In a 2006 report Musser and O'Reilly speak of it as "a set of economic, social, and technology trends that collectively form the basis for the next generation of the Internet". However, some people argue that Web 2.0 is merely a meaningless marketing buzzword (Brodkin 2007). It seems necessary to further illuminate it and its context in order to come up with a definition of the concept.

In 2004, the term gained popularity when O'Reilly Media and MediaLive initiated the first Web 2.0 conference (O'Reilly 2007). O'Reilly and others (Hoegg et al. 2006; McAfee 2006; Vossen & Hagemann 2007) came up with a number of general principles describing the properties of Web 2.0. Knol, Spruit and Scheper (2008) compared the principles proposed by different authors and proposed a generic set of Web 2.0 principles (they refer to them as Social Computing principles) that are depicted by the nine circles in Figure 1.

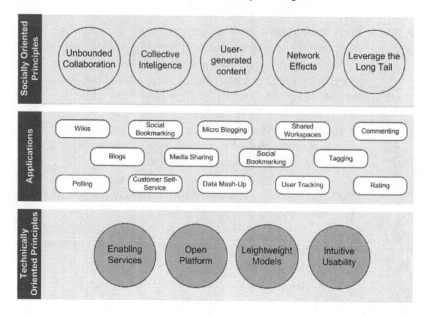

Figure 1: Web 2.0 principles (adopted from Knol et al., 2008) and popular applications

Knol et al. (2008) point out that the four principles in the bottom of Figure 1 are technically oriented and provide the fundament for the five socially oriented principles in the top. We argue that the phenomenon of Web 2.0, i.e. what you can see about it, can be mainly related to the socially oriented principles that are enabled by a set of Web 2.0 Technologies. Therefore, we propose the following definitions based on the Web 2.0 principles:

Web 2.0 is the reorientation of the Web that promotes unbounded interaction, collaboration and participation of people. It is characterized by the emergence of a large amount of content generated by a collective of Internet users. It harnesses networking effects and leverages the long tail.

Web 2.0 Technologies are technologies that transform the Web into a platform spanning all connected devices. They enable the creation of web-services and applications, constructed from lightweight models, and can be used intuitively.

Some examples of Web 2.0 Technologies are AJAX and lightweight script-ing languages like PHP, Perl, Python and Ruby (Andersen 2007).

By reviewing literature (Chui et al. 2009; Andersen 2007; Knol 2008) we identified a number of common, but certainly not all, Web 2.0 applications, services and techniques (in the following only referred to as Web 2.0 appli-cations). They are depicted in the middle layer of Figure 1. We added "Mi-cro-Blogging" (e.g. Twitter) as application since we think that this consid-erably new trend can be valuable for KM as explained later.

2.3 Enterprise 2.0

Applying Web 2.0 principles on companies is widely referred to as Enter-prise 2.0 (McAfee 2006; Tredinnick 2006; Levy 2009). Levy reviewed litera-ture dealing with Enterprise 2.0 and proposes a matrix (Figure 2) that structures Enterprise 2.0 according to two dimensions: the type of tech-nology used and the type of user that is being addressed.

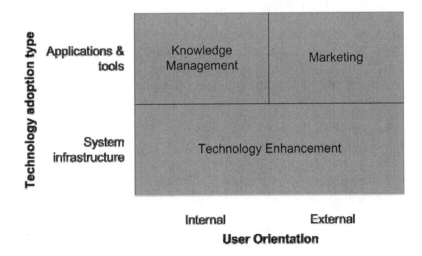

Figure 2: Enterprise 2.0 segments (adapted from Levy, 2009)

The "technology adoption type" dimension distinguishes between two types of adoption: Web 2.0 system infrastructure (developing in light-weight models, using AJAX etc.), which can be related to the technological aspect of Web 2.0 as introduced in the previous section; and secondly Web 2.0 applications and tools (using wikis, blogs, tagging etc.), which stem from the phenomenon aspect of Web 2.0.

The "user orientation" dimension distinguishes between the use of these technologies with an internal (by and for the organization) and an external focus (facing customers, suppliers and other external stakeholders). As suggested by the matrix in Figure 2, KM enabled by Web 2.0 principles is one specific aspect of Enterprise 2.0 that encompasses an internal focus together with adoption of Web 2.0 applications and tools.

This raises the question which Web 2.0 applications have an impact on KM. Are they just an enhancement of KM practices by a number of fancy tools or do they pave the way for of new kind of KM, a KM 2.0? By conducting case studies in two student-run organizations why attempt to answer this question.

3   Cases studies

Due to the exploratory nature of the research question case study research (CSR) was chosen as the principal research method. CSR is a research method that is applicable in situations where a number of variables are to be observed in a real life context and where this observation cannot simply be limited to an analysis of data points (Yin 2008: 18). It can involve both qualitative and quantitative evidence and is especially applicable to real-life situations that are too complex for survey and experimental research (Yin 2008: 19).

In order to explore how Web 2.0 can be used for KM we studied two student organizations. The analysis was divided into three steps:

Analyze the KM function using Binney's KM spectrum;

Determine which technology, especially in regards to Web 2.0, is used to support specific elements of the KM spectrum;

Provide recommendations regarding the potential of Web 2.0 applications for KM.

A recent study published by Pew Research Institute shows that the largest group of people using the Internet, in fact, consists of people born between 1977 and 1990 (Jones & Fox 2009). In a 2009 article on Web 2.0's implications on KM, Levy proposes to use the young generation as pioneers of Web 2.0 in organizations to leverage KM practices. Obviously, the generation of today's students is the most active group of Internet users and thus most familiar with the new technologies of Web 2.0. We therefore think that student-run organizations are an interesting subject for researching the implications of Web 2.0 on KM practices.

The case studies involved a number of semi-structured interviews with key personnel and a review of IS fragments of AIESEC in Germany and MARKET TEAM, which are two of Germany's largest student-run organizations. Prior to carrying out research we developed a case study protocol that described field procedures and the principal questions to be answered.

Both organizations are non-profit organizations (NPOs) and are run by student volunteers on the local level and students working fulltime on the national level. In general, people change position every year which makes knowledge retention a key challenge. As in the NPO domain in general, knowledge in the two organizations can be classified into accounting / administrative, managerial / organizational, teaching / training, fund raising / public relation management / marketing, operational and miscellaneous knowledge (Lettieri et al. 2004).

Both organizations are at different stages of adopting Web 2.0 technologies to enhance their KM practices. Due to their different size and scope (national vs. international) they also differ considerably in regard to their KM needs as indicated by Hume & Hume (2008).

3.1 MARKET TEAM

MARKET TEAM e.V. (in the following MT), solely operating in Germany, aims at providing students insights into the business world by organizing events like workshops, trainings and symposia with companies. The organization has around 1000 members in 23 chapters (Market Team 2010). KM aims at supporting day to day operations of the organization, which mainly consist of running various projects on both the local and the national level. In general, KM takes place on the local level. There is no knowledge sharing between different chapters. At the moment the organization runs an initiative that aims at improving knowledge sharing between local chapters to build on synergy effect, i.e. re-use knowledge in different parts of the organization.

We analyzed MT's KM function using Binney's (2001) KM spectrum and identified the aspects shown in the upper part of Figure 3 we listed the web applications used to support these KM aspects.

In the past ten years MT has been using a custom developed web platform for fostering communication between the national board and the chapters, for administering member data, for exchanging information and experiences about completed projects and for storing information about partner companies. Since the platform is mainly designed for unilateral communication from national to local level, the organization is currently evaluating how it can be replaced by a more interactive platform leveraging Web 2.0 technologies.

Some local chapters use wiki platforms based on MediaWiki for facilitating project management. In general, information and experience report from previous projects and manuals how to run a project are retrieved from the national web platform and the local platform is used mainly for facilitating communication and collaboration between the members of project teams. In addition they may guide project teams through the process of running a project.

Besides physical meetings, communication mainly takes place through emails but also through StudiVZ, a large German social networking platform. These channels are therefore the main mean of exchange ideas and contributing to innovation.

Skill development and training solely takes place in physical meetings and apart from providing manuals and explicit information on the national web platform, no specific web technology is used for this aspect of KM.

	Transactional	Analytical	Asset Management	Process	Developmental	Innovation and Creation
KM Applications	• Help Desk Applications	• Customer Relationship Management (CRM)	• Document Management • Knowledge Reporsitories • Content Management	• Best practises • Quality Management • Process Automation	• Skills Development • Staff Competencies • Learning • Teaching • Training	• Communities • Collaboration • Discussion Forums • Networking • Virtual Teams • Multi-disciplined Teams
Web 2.0 Applications			• Media Wiki • Dropbox			• Media Wiki • StudiVZ • Mindmeister • Google Spreadsheets • Google Docs

Figure 3: KM and Web 2.0 applications used for KM by MT

Following the general trend, members have started using free Web 2.0 tools for collaborating and sharing files with each other. Dropbox is mainly used for sharing and storing documents online. Google Docs and Spreadsheets and Mindmeister, an online mind map tool, are used for collaboration and idea generation. These tools were not specifically introduced by the organization, but just appeared to be useful and very often already known by members from personal use.

3.2 AIESEC Germany

AIESEC has over 45,000 members globally (AIESEC International 2009), whereof more than 2,500 are from 47 chapters in Germany. The organization aims at developing tomorrow's socially responsible leaders by running an integrated leadership development program and providing coordinating internships at its partner companies around the world (AIESEC International 2009). Due to its size and international scope AIESEC's KM is directed at leveraging economies of scale by providing one single web platform connecting members from around the world. In accordance with Hume and Hume (2008) KM in general can be considered operationally and strategically mature and KM structures try to capture both explicit and tacit knowledge. A key challenge of AIESEC's KM is to find the best KM approach that fits all the different cultures and national branches' needs (size differs significantly reaching from a few dozen to thousands of members in some countries). Therefore, KM programs are mainly run on the national level, although making it available to the global network is also a concern.

In 2007, the national executive board of AIESEC Germany decided to foster the vision of a "member driven organization", i.e. a bottom-up organization that benefits from the contribution of every single member. In order to achieve this from a KM perspective steps have been taken to adopt Web 2.0 applications such as wikis to enable every member to contribute to the organizational knowledge base. Since then the organization has adopted a number of Web 2.0 applications to improve collaboration and knowledge sharing between its members. The upper part of Figure 4 provides an overview of different KM aspects in AIESEC Germany and the bottom part shows Web 2.0 applications used for supporting these aspects.

	Transactional	Analytical	Asset Management	Process	Developmental	Innovation and Creation
KM Applications	• Help Desk Applications	• Customer Relationship Management (CRM) • Business Intelligence	• Document Management • Knowledge Repositories • Content Management	• Best practises • Quality Management • Process Automation	• Skills Development • Staff Competencies • Learning • Teaching • Training	• Communities • Collaboration • Discussion Forums • Networking • Virtual Teams • Multi-disciplined Teams
Web 2.0 Applications		• Google Analytics • Google Forms • Tagging	• Web Portal • OpenCMS • Google Video • Youtube • Flickr • Wikis	• Brandkore	• Google Presentation • Slide Share • Google Video • WizIQ • Teamviewer • Meetgreen	• Google Spreadsheet • Google Docs • Google Calendar • Mind42 • Goggle Mail • Goggle Talk • Skype • Facebook • Blogspot • Twitter • Wikis

Figure 4: KM and Web 2.0 applications used for KM by AIESEC

Germany

AIESEC's global web platform contains a wiki module in which every user can create wiki pages. Two years ago, AIESEC Germany has switched from a Lotus Domino powered knowledge base to providing knowledge assets in these wiki pages. Information in AIESEC's global web platform is searchable through an advanced search function based on tags and elaborated filters. These wikis are used for storing information such as manuals, contain processes documentations and are used for collaborative idea generation (e.g. virtual brainstorming sessions). Even though wikis should enable everybody to contribute content or enrich other people's contributions, only a limited number of members have actually been doing it and most of them are nationally active. Since there were some problems with the usability of the platform when it was launched, an interviewee supposed that the problem might be related to that.

AIESEC recently started using Google Apps, a bundle of collaborative web applications. Its word processing module and its spreadsheets module are mainly used for documentation (e.g. minutes) and idea generation (e.g. brainstorming). The presentation module is used for virtual education and the video module is used to distribute education videos. A module that allows for creating forms that is used for creating surveys amongst members. In addition, for improving interaction and information exchange between the members a webmail application and a built-in instant messaging client that is identical with Google's consumer product Gmail is used. According to an interviewee the acceptance of Google Apps was significantly facilitated by its intuitive interface and the fact that users already knew the applications from personal use.

In order to streamline their marketing material creation, which needs to be customized for each chapter, AIESEC uses Brandkore, a web-based marketing automation tool. Consequently, members do not need to be familiar with using complicated graphic suits anymore

In order to facilitate the development and learning of its members AIESEC uses a number of e-learning applications such as the platform WizIQ and Teamviewer in combination with web-controlled telephone conferencing tools such as Meetgreen. The organization is currently evaluating the use of web-based video conferencing tools such as Netviewer that allow multiple users to see and interact with each other.

In order to keep members up to date a news module and a classifieds module in the global web platform of AIESEC are used. In addition, a public Google Calendar is used to inform members about upcoming events. Although some communication channels such as Facebook and Twitter are intended for communication with external stakeholders, members have started using them for internal communications and collaboration amongst each other as well.

4 Discussion

The two case studies show that Web 2.0 applications can be used for KM. When we look at Binney's KM spectrum and the Web 2.0 applications matched with the respective elements (see Figure 3 and 4), we notice that apparently not all elements of the spectrum are associated with Web 2.0 applications.

We used the findings from the case studies to derive a number of generic Web 2.0 applications (as those in Figure 1) and mapped them to the KM spectrum. The result is shown in Figure 5.

We added some applications (italic font type in Figure 5) to the ones that we found in the case studies since we found some evidence in literature that they can be used for KM. Hideo and Shinichi (2007) describe how communication data generated from Web 2.0 applications such as social networking platforms can be used to create new knowledge. Chui et al. (2009) note that data from social bookmarking and ratings can be used for creating additional information. Anderson (2007) describes how podcasts can be used for educational purposes. We did not derive a generic Web 2.0 application from Brandkore that we identified in the AIESEC case because we think that is an applications that mainly builds on the technological enhancement aspect of Web 2.0 and cannot be related to any socially oriented Web 2.0 principle.

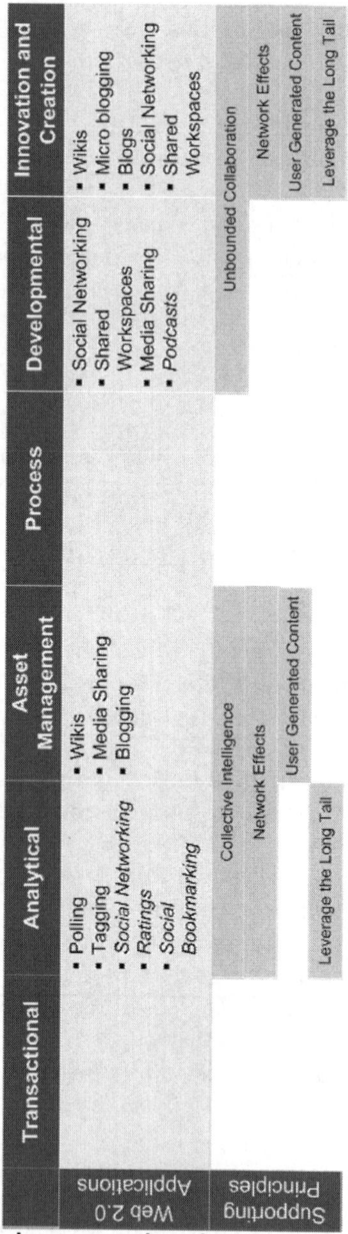

	Transactional	Analytical	Asset Management	Process	Developmental	Innovation and Creation
Web 2.0 Applications		▪ Polling ▪ Tagging ▪ *Social Networking* ▪ *Ratings* ▪ *Social Bookmarking*	▪ Wikis ▪ Media Sharing ▪ Blogging		▪ Social Networking ▪ Shared Workspaces ▪ Media Sharing ▪ *Podcasts*	▪ Wikis ▪ Micro blogging ▪ Blogs ▪ Social Networking ▪ Shared Workspaces
Supporting Principles		Collective Intelligence Network Effects User Generated Content Leverage the Long Tail			Unbounded Collaboration Network Effects User Generated Content Leverage the Long Tail	

Figure 5: Web 2.0 principles mapped to the KM spectrum

In a second step we used the mapping of Web 2.0 applications to associate the socially oriented Web 2.0 principles with the elements of the KM spectrum.

We added some applications (italic font type in Figure 5) to the ones that we found in the case studies since we found some evidence in literature that they can be used for KM. Hideo and Shinichi (2007) describe how communication data generated from Web 2.0 applications such as social networking platforms can be used to create new knowledge. Chui et al. (2009) note that data from social bookmarking and ratings can be used for creating additional information. Anderson (2007) describes how podcasts can be used for educational purposes. We did not derive a generic Web 2.0 application from Brandkore that we identified in the AIESEC case because we think that is an applications that mainly builds on the technological enhancement aspect of Web 2.0 and cannot be related to any socially oriented Web 2.0 principle.

In a second step we used the mapping of Web 2.0 applications to associate the socially oriented Web 2.0 principles with the elements of the KM spectrum.

"Collective Intelligence" refers to the fact that a large collective can create more content than a small number of experts (Knol et al. 2008) and that intelligence can be derived from data created by a large number of users (Anderson 2007: 41). This applies to analytical KM and asset management. Analytical KM applications may create information from large amounts of user data such as social bookmarking and ratings. Wikis, as an asset management tool, also rely on this principle because their content may be created by large numbers of users whereof everyone just contributes a small amount.

"Network Effects" refer to services that get better, the more people use them (Knol et al. 2008). This applies to basically all analytical KM applications that we identified. Also the content of wikis and other asset management applications benefits from network effects. Finally, also network effects are also relevant to social networking and micro blogging that are related to innovation and creation KM.

"User Generated Content" refers to the large amount of content that is generated by users (Knol et al. 2008). This content may be stored in asset management applications such as wikis, blogs or media sharing platforms. The fact that users generate content also leads to an increased creation of ideas and innovation. However, it should be noted that quality of content might become an issue in comparison with traditional KM approaches where content is mainly generated by a small number of experts. Apart from that there might be a risk of a low user participation in content creation (Tredinnick 2006). This issue is clearly linked to organizational culture. Consequently, only certain types of organizations may benefit from user generated content. Tredinnick (2006) suggests that especially dynamic organization in a fast changing environment and built on a high degree of innovation may benefit from this aspect of Web 2.0.

"Leverage the long tail", i.e. the exploration of niches (Knol et al. 2008), applied to micro blogging and social networking services may be beneficial for knowledge creation in such a way that users may exchange snippets of information that they would otherwise not have known about. These micro messages may lead to creation of new ideas and innovations. In addition, we think that analytical KM might also benefit from the long tail in such a way that the interaction of users can be used as an additional source for data mining as suggested by Hideo and Shinichi (2007).

"Unbounded collaboration" refers to a form of collaboration that is independent from place and time, i.e. time differences and different locations do not matter anymore. It enables creativity processes that were not possible before. Furthermore, this novel kind of collaboration might also lead to cost and time savings because travel might be reduced. This also has an impact on training and education because e-learning and virtual conferencing applications may be used.

This discussion shows that Web 2.0 applications may be beneficial to four elements of Binney's (2001) KM spectrum, i.e. analytical KM, asset management, developmental KM and innovation and creation. Although transactional and process-oriented KM does not seem to benefit from Web 2.0 applications, it may benefit from enhancing technology by adopting technical principles. For instance, the AIESEC case suggests that intuitiveness is a key enabler for the acceptance of a new technology.

In the case of AIESEC we have also found out that there does not seem to be such a clear differentiation between internal and external use of Web 2.0 applications as proposed by Levy (2009) (see Figure 2) because organizational members communicate about internal subjects in open channels, e.g. social networking sites. This overlap of internal and external communication might become a real problem for the organization by decreasing the attractiveness of public relation campaigns and by making confidential information available to public. We assume that one possible reason for this blend of communication could be that organizational members do not find the communication channels that they desire to use inside the organizations. By introducing and fostering internal social networking platforms organizations may mitigate this issue.

5 Conclusions

The research question, as proposed in section 1, states:

How can organizations use Web 2.0 applications for managing knowledge and which impact do they have on KM?

We conducted exploratory case study research in two study-run organizations to explore in how they use Web 2.0 applications for different aspects of their KM strategy. Based on the findings we were able to identify which aspects of KM, as described in Binney's (2001) KM spectrum, benefit from Web 2.0 applications. As a last step we created a generic KM spectrum for Web 2.0 applications.

The research suggests that analytical KM, asset management, developmental KM and innovation & creation may benefit from the adoption of Web 2.0 applications. Depending on the organizational culture these applications may even lead to a novel kind of KM. This new approach to KM would not just benefit from a technology enhancement of the existing applications, but also lead to a new understanding of KM that is based on user contributions, a novel way of unbounded collaboration and leveraging the long tail of user interaction data. In our opinion, it would therefore be appropriate to refer to this as KM 2.0.

The findings in this research are based on two case studies. To expand external validity of the findings research should be extended by replicating the case study in different types of organizations. It would be interesting to have a look at other types of non-profit organizations and for-profit organizations and examine if there are considerable differences in term of KM and the impact of Web 2.0 applications. The framework proposed in Figure 6 can be used for providing recommendations to organizations that intent adopting Web 2.0 applications for bolstering up KM. Therefore, the applicability as a tool for providing recommendations should also be tested.

As we observed a low participation in wikis in one of the cases (AIESEC) and no knowledge sharing between different chapters of the other organization (MT), we suppose that organizational culture and structure have a major effect on the effectiveness of adopting Web 2.0 applications for KM. Further research should therefore investigate the influence of organizational culture and other factors on the effectiveness of adopting Web 2.0 applications for KM.

References

AIESEC International (2009) "Welcome to AIESEC International", [online], http://www.aiesec.org/cms/aiesec/AI/students/index.html.

Andersen, P. (2007) What is Web 2.0?: ideas, technologies and implications for education, JISC, London.

Binney, D., (2001) "The knowledge management spectrum-understanding the KM landscape", *Journal of Knowledge Management*, Vol 5, No. 1, pp. 33-42.

Brodkin, J. (2007) "Web 2.0: Buzzword, or Internet revolution?", [online], Network World, http://www.networkworld.com/news/2007/012407-web-20.html.

Chui, M., Miller, A. & Roberts, R.P. (2009) "Six ways to make Web 2.0 work", *The McKinsey Quarterly*, February, pp. 1-7.

Dalkir, K. (2005) *Knowledge management in theory and practice*, Elsevier Butterworth-Heinemann, Burlington, MA, USA.

Davenport, T.H., De Long, D.W. & Beers, M.C. (1999) "Successful knowledge management projects", *The Knowledge Management Yearbook 1999-2000*, Elsevier Butterworth-Heinemann, Burlington, MA, USA.

Dul, J. & Hak, T. (2008) *Case study methodology in business research*, Elsevier Butterworth-Heinemann, Burlington, MA, USA.

Hideo, S. & Shinichi, K. (2007). KM 2.0: Business Knowledge Sharing in the Web 2.0 Age. *NEC Technical Journal*, Vol 2, No. 2, pp. 50-54.

Hoegg, R. et al. (2006) "Overview of business models for Web 2.0 communities", *Proceedings of GeNeMe*, 2006, pp. 23-37.

Hume, C. & Hume, M. (2008) "The strategic role of knowledge management in nonprofit organisations", *International Journal of Nonprofit and Voluntary Sector Marketing*, Vol 13, No. 2, pp. 129-140.

Jashapara, A. (2004) *Knowledge management: an integrated approach*, Pearson Education, Essex, UK.

Jones, S. & Fox, S. (2009). "Generational Differences in Online Activities", [online], Pew Internet & American Life Project, http://www.pewinternet.org/Reports/2009/Generations-Online-in-2009/Generational-Differences-in-Online-Activities.aspx?r=1.

Knol, P., Spruit, M. & Scheper, W. (2008) "Web 2.0 Revealed - Business Model Innovation through Social Computing", *Proceedings of the Seventh AIS SIGeBIZ Workshop on e-business*.

Lettieri, E., Borga, F. & Savoldelli, A. (2004) "Knowledge management in non-profit organizations", *Journal of Knowledge Management*, Vol 8, No. 6, pp. 16-30.

Levy, M. (2009) "WEB 2.0 implications on knowledge management", *Journal of Knowledge Management*, Vol 13, No. 1, pp. 120-134.

Market Team (2010) "MARKET TEAM e.V. - Die fachübergreifende Studeninitiative", [online], http://www.market-team.de/national/.

McAfee, A.P. (2006) "Enterprise 2.0: The dawn of emergent collaboration", *MIT Sloan Management Review*, Vol 47, No 3, pp. 21-28.

Musser, T. & O'Reilly, T. (2006) "Web 2.0 Principles and Best Practices", [online], http://radar.oreilly.com/research/web2-report.html.

O'Reilly, T. (2007) "What Is Web 2.0: Design Patterns and Business Models for the Next Generation of Software", *Communications & Strategies*, Vol 65, pp. 17-37.

Tredinnick, L. (2006) "Web 2.0 and Business: A pointer to the intranets of the future?", *Business Information Review*, Vol 3, No. 4, pp. 228-234.

Vossen, G. & Hagemann, S. (2007) *Unleashing Web 2.0: From concepts to creativity*, Elsevier Morgan-Kaufmann, Boston, USA.

Yin, R.K. (2008) *Case Study Research: Design and Methods,* 4th edition, Sage, Thousand Oaks, USA.

To Tweet or not to Tweet, that is the Question – Social Media as a Missed Opportunity for Knowledge Management

Tim Wright[1], Stuart Watson[2], Daniela Castrataro[2]
[1]Tescape, Glasgow, UK
[2]Intellectual Assets Centre, Glasgow, UK
Originally published in the Proceedings of ECKM 2010

Editorial Commentary

In this paper, the authors reveal through a survey, that the KM community are not leading the adoption of Social Media. They speculate on the reasons for this. First, the community are not convinced of the value of Social Media. Second, they may feel the application of Social Media is in areas outside of their domain. And third, they feel unable to make a compelling business case for adoption within their organizations. I too am surprised by the lack of uptake by the KM community though I am not so sure of the reasons. I suspect it's more likely that the KM community has not taken the time to experiment with Social Tools and have yet to fully appreciate their potential.

Abstract: As individuals and as social agents, many have embraced Social Media (SM), the benefits of which are self-apparent and are taken for granted within the context of this paper. Evidence would suggest that the penetration and demographic spread of the adoption of SM continues to grow rapidly within our daily life, not only on a personal level, but also in the workplace. However, there is a lack of research relating to SM and its application within specific business areas. Firstly, this paper intends to focus on the utilisation of SM to foster Knowledge Management (KM) potential within organisations. Anecdotally, an important concern of decision makers is the reputational risk and threat to traditional models of Intellectual Property management posed by the use of SM in the workplace. In addition, there is a perception that the business use of social networking websites is "time wasting" and not cost-effective, considering the perceived resource requirements to manage and successfully exploit the phenomenon of SM. However, within organisations, there are a range of stakeholders that could potentially play an important role in influencing decision makers' views in terms of limiting the risk and gaining the business opportunities which SM offers. The authors believe that SM can offer tremendous benefits and opportunities for knowledge-aware management, including new knowledge creation, fresh approaches to Intellectual Property generation and innovation, and the development of valuable and deep insights into client and customer perception. Each of the aforementioned opportunities may result in commercial benefits and advantages. But, in the absence of clear and compelling models for the application and exploitation of SM, the uptake of these tools could remain patchy, and the potential for KM practitioners to influence decision makers, regarding focusing on the positive side of the risk/opportunity equation, will be challenging. Secondly, the result of this paper is to improve the understanding of businesses perception and adoption of SM and the role of KM in that. The authors devised a survey that sought to capture the scope and nature of the use of SM in a business context, the application areas of work to which it is being applied, the key champions for the use of SM and the key constraints and guidance on its use. In particular, the authors aimed to gain insight into an organisation's perspectives regarding the opportunities and threats offered by SM for the generation of Intellectual Assets and especially of new knowledge. The intent was to gain an "as is" view and identify commonalities that have resulted in a positive perception of SM. The paper presents the findings of this survey, identifying the key applications of SM, where it is implemented and utilised, the prevailing attitudes and the key influencer for decision makers. In addition, the results specifically intend to demonstrate the active or passive role of the KM community in the wider business application of SM, highlighting areas where the authors believe opportunity exists for KM practitioners to influence decisions through a more extensive use of SM.

Keywords: Social Media, Social Networking, Knowledge Management, Strategic Decision Making, Crowdsourcing, Co-creation, Innovation, Web 2.0

1   Introduction

The penetration and demographic spread of the adoption of Social Media (SM) continues to grow rapidly. For example, within the past year, access to Twitter by UK users alone has increased by 974% (Goad, 2009); and with more than 400 million active users, Facebook would be the 4th largest "country" in the world whilst Generation Y will outnumber Boomers by

2010 as the largest generational group with 96% participating in social networks. Nevertheless some ask, is social media a fad? Or is it the biggest shift since the Industrial Revolution?" (Socialnomics, 2009). Undoubtedly this has been a comparatively rapid change. It took 38 years for the radio to reach 50 million users, whereas Facebook added 100 million users in 9 months (Socialnomics, 2009). Social Media has already attracted a great deal of interest in the business community, not all of it positive. There are organisations that are readily embracing aspects of this phenomenon whilst others are yet to be convinced of its business value even believing many of its more commonly cited applications as little more than a waste of time. Nevertheless the recent AIIM Survey of Social Media Activists (AIIM, 2010; Mancini, 2010) suggests that 30% of its respondents use Twitter, which for the cynics represents one of the most frivolous of SM tools, for business networking at least once per day. The authors believe SM has a valuable role to play in business and therefore sought to understand patterns of adoption of SM in business, and in particular to establish which groups, if they could be identified, were leading the charge to introduce it. The proposition to use SM in Knowledge Management (KM) initiatives seems, to us at least, to be a very compelling one and we were curious to see if the KM community shared that view and if they were in fact at the forefront, or perceived to be at the forefront, of the introduction of SM, within a business context. Our approach to the question was to configure a questionnaire that could be completed online and encouraged participants from all sectors and geographic regions to participate.

This paper intends to focus on the perception and utilisation of SM in business organisations and to understand the role in relation to KM. There are a range of stakeholders that could play an important role in influencing decision makers' views of SM in business. The authors believe that SM can offer tremendous benefits and opportunities for knowledge-aware management, including new knowledge creation, fresh approaches to Intellectual Property generation and innovation, and the development of valuable and deep insights into client and customer perception. Each of the aforementioned opportunities may result in commercial benefit and advantage. However, the authors accept that in the absence of clear and compelling models for the application and exploitation of SM, the uptake of these tools could remain patchy, and that the potential for KM practitioners to influence decision makers to focus on the positive side of the risk/opportunity equation of SM will be challenging.

This paper identifies key findings of the survey results which seem to indicate missed opportunities for the KM community and highlights some of the more striking and curious metrics. We will consider where SM tools could have significant application in the KM domain, at the same time considering briefly some suggested reasons for the apparent lack of KM exploitation of these opportunities as they appear to the authors.

2 Methodology

To ascertain the business adoption of SM, a questionnaire was created and advertised online[1], through Social Networks and by emailing individuals. The findings for this paper are based on the initial six-week post-launch period between February and March 2010. The survey sought to obtain data on how businesses generally use and manage SM and in particular how it is used to maximise the value of their Intellectual Assets and how they deal with Intellectual Property issues involved in the use of SM. The questionnaire contained twenty-one questions; a mixed methodological approach was devised with both open and multiple choice questions. Businesses were evaluated on different levels, reflecting the three sections of the questionnaire: Awareness and Use of Social Media; Intellectual Property Considerations; Intellectual Assets Considerations. Within these holistic topics, a number of questions related to the management of knowledge within the organisations. The resulting number of respondents for first six-week sample was 134, since there was no canvassing of possible respondents, it is difficult to explicitly state the response rate. However, the response number was favourable in comparison to similar sized surveys surrounding this subject matter (Journalism.co.uk, 2010).

3 General findings

In the recent AIIM, Survey of Social Media Activists (AIIM, 2010;Mancini, 2010) taken in February 2010, 76% of respondents agreed either strongly or very strongly with statement "I think that business social networking tools help me to do my job better" and 62% felt that "it's becoming increasingly important for my job that I am active on social networks".

---

[1] http://www.surveymonkey.com/s/socialmediaquestionnaire

In conducting our survey, we identified a number of points which support and refute general perceptions of the use of social media within the business context. The majority of companies (86.3%) are using SM in the workplace for work-related purposes. Of the companies who responded to our survey, the prevalent usage of SM is social networking, with an overwhelming 81.9% of respondents using websites such as Facebook, LinkedIn and Bebo. Over half of respondents noted that social networking websites were used for networking with individuals external to the organisation, however the focus was upon using social networks for Hiring (63.1%) and Marketing (61.2%). Also, the usage of blogs (48%), Microblogging such as Twitter (49%) and Wikis (46.1%) was high. A number of respondents declared use of Livecasting/Instant Messaging tools and Video Sharing. The responses to the survey also outlined a large use of employment website (26.5%) for recruitment purposes. The use of SM for hiring may stem from organisations sourcing new talent or identifying the skills in the external workforce. Conversely it could also be argued that individuals were using SM at work to source future potential employment. Without further research, this question will be left unanswered. The use of SM monitoring tools (i.e. Social Radar) and Crowd sourcing tools, whilst relatively low should not perhaps be ignored even with such a relatively small pool of respondents.

41% of companies have used these tools for more than 2 years and a total of 68% have been using them for between 1 and 2 years. 74% of responses stated that all staff are allowed access to SM within the work place for work related purposes. Only 10.8% answered "Only Managers" as a select group permitted to use SM in the workplace. This apparent lack of constraint seems to go against anecdotal evidence. An overwhelming 71.1% have not introduced policies and/or guidelines for conducting business practice online, another statistic which is surprising as it juxtaposed to a survey carried out by CloudNet (Journalism.co.uk, 2010) which identified that only 20% of respondents did not have a social media policy implemented. It should be noted that CloudNet's survey size was similar to ours. Our survey identified that the majority of individuals did not have concerns with disclosing their company's intellectual property (76.3%) through the use of SM. However, according to the UK IPO (2009), when an employee discloses information regarding a company innovation on a SM website such as Facebook, Twitter and or Flickr, this could invalidate a potential patent application, therefore the resultant risk of disclosure so could be severe to certain businesses.

61.2% of respondents stated that the majority of the use of SM is for marketing purposes, for example, many use Twitter for raising brand awareness. A large percentage of respondents believe that SM helps to exploit their Intellectual Assets (IA), but what appears to be implied by IA is little beyond Brand Awareness/Recognition. Many respondents also declared the use SM to interact and analyse their customers. There seems to be little differentiation between public and private sector, again challenging expectations and anecdotal evidence. Those differences that can be found are largely in the tools in use by each sector: the private sector seems to use Microblogging more than formal blogging and, generally speaking, the private sector appears to use a greater variety of tools.

4 KM observations

The findings of the survey are interesting to the authors as it appears to suggest that KM practitioners are not, or are not perceived to be, in the vanguard of championing the adoption of SM tools within a business context. In addition, the potentially powerful applications that SM tools offer to the KM domain do not appear to be embedded or necessarily understood. Given the sample size, we have focused mainly on the broader indicators avoiding granular analysis. As the survey remains open, we hope that over time, the sample size will increase, and that will allow us to investigate specific sectoral and geographic comparisons. However, even the broad indicators present cause for thought and reflection by the KM community.

It is striking that when asked about the key groups championing the use of SM for work related purposes within their workplace, the clear leaders in pushing for its use are the Marketing and Communications (Marcomms) group by some marked degree. In both Public and Private sector groups, around 25% felt that Marcomms were the key players in introducing and championing the use of SM. If Sales is added to this group, then the results are even more compelling as 17.5% felt Sales were, or are, the key champions. KM came in at 11.3% and, within the public sector, even behind the IT group. This was particularly surprising given the anecdotal evidence that suggests IT stakeholders are commonly seen as a blocker to the adoption of SM. However, it is striking that defined KM practitioners are not perceived to be at the forefront of pushing for the adoption of SM in the workplace.

This appears even more surprising when one considers that more than 50% of respondents saw SM as valuable for managing the intellectual assets of their company. We can quite reasonably regard Intellectual Assets (IA) as being knowledge assets and typically an area for the involvement of KM professionals. Yet this stands at odds with the efforts of KM staff to be seen as champions of SM. If we dig a little deeper, however, we learn that few respondents considered IA as being more than brand awareness and recognition, and with this rather limited perspective of what constitutes IA, it is hardly surprising that the Marketers, the traditional custodians of brand management, are at the heart of SM activities.

Less than 50% declare they use Wikis in the workplace and less than 25% marked the use of social bookmarking. This seems surprising given the high usage of SM generally and the anecdotal high visibility of wiki based tools such as Wikipedia. If we set this alongside the finding of the AIIM survey (AIIM, 2010; Mancini, 2010), where 71% agreed with the statement that they would be "willing to participate in a wiki or other tool to gather together and share best practices", one wonders why the take up of this opportunity seems relatively low. Of course what people say they "will do" and what they actually "do" are quite different things.

One interesting finding – again when compared to anecdotal evidence – was the apparent low levels of use of SM applications for internal KM initiatives. This seems surprising given that the majority of respondents classed themselves as working for organisations of more than 250 staff where the opportunity for deployment of SM tools for internal KM application must be stronger than in smaller organisations. However, by a ratio of nearly 2:1, respondents stated knowledge sharing is conducted with external parties rather than internally. However the use of SM for external knowledge exchange may be no bad thing. In the recently published European Innovation Scoreboard (Pro Inno Europe, 2009), it was found that more than half of firms classed as innovating firms involved users (i.e. external parties) in their innovation efforts. These were described in the survey as "super innovators". This could be the by-product of one or both of the following: 1. Employees believe that knowledge gained through analysing the external environment will be of more benefit to the organisation; or 2. KM using SM focuses upon the identification of explicit knowledge, whereas tacit knowledge (if you accept these definitions) created/shared internally is shared through interaction and/or collaboration within the interaction of IT, specifically SM. Our survey found that 16% of companies declare they use SM for crowd-sourcing purposes which could well include the involvement of users in innovation activities and so is broadly in keeping with the European Innovation Scoreboard (2009) findings. However, we should restate that it is those coming from a Marcomms background that are leading the uptake of SM, it could be a cause for concern for KM practitioners if it were the Marcomms teams who were pushing businesses into the "super innovator" category.

4.1 Social Media missed opportunities in the KM domain

In the view of the authors, SM presents tremendous opportunities in the KM domain. Whilst we understand that KM has a range of definitions that fill a broad spectrum, ranging from those believing that it is little more than an extension of information management through to those that feel it represents a radical and holistic management agenda aimed at nurturing and harnessing human cognition for business advantage, SM still has something to offer. We are not alone in this view. The IFLA conference of 2008 (Dysart, 2008) apparently had SM as one of its three key conference threads, and even a casual review of KM literature will find many references to the importance and impact of SM. This view is confirmed by Tapscott and Williams who posited the idea of the New Alexandrians in Wikinomics (Tapscot & Williams, 2007), an idea that one would expect to resonate with even the most conservative in the KM domain. The former Forrester researchers and authors Li and Bernoff (2008) agree by emphasising in their book Grounswell how SM underpins a landscape changed by the wikinomics revolution. In addition, companies may benefit from SM instruments for enhancing knowledge processing, which is (to some) the essential aim of KM, as Joe Firestone, CEO of Knowledge Management Consortium International, states:

"SM tools enable increased: social networking, connectivity, distributed content creation and aggregation, self-organisation, and col-

*laboration. They may, also, if introduced into a social system, en-
hance aspects of knowledge processing including problem seeking,
recognition and formulation; creating new knowledge; and knowledge integration. And that's why KM may want to introduce SM
tools or support others in introducing them. The democratisation of
content production in the context of more intense social interaction,
promised and, arguably, produced by SM tools, is something that
KM should seek and support."* (Firestone, 2009)

If marketers are making the most of externally facing SM, KM is certainly
missing the best opportunities when it comes to their exploitation within
the firewall. One compelling case of an internally faced "social KM strategy" is IBM's. IBM have developed an integrated social software package
for business rather than a strategy, which has been tested by IBM employees (IBM, 2007). Lotus Connection, IBM's trading name for the suite, includes a comprehensive suite of SM tools and applications for internal social networking: blogs, social bookmarking and communities. Their intent
in developing this tool suite was to enhance knowledge processing within
their organisation. The internal social network is extremely useful for finding and meeting with the "right" people throughout the company. Blogs
could allow for increased knowledge transfer and collaborative idea generation across the enterprise. The shared bookmarking system in a company intranet site, with access to both internet and intranet resources, is
in this case connected to the enterprise directory through the use of tags,
thus allowing again to find the people with the right expertise within a
specific domain. The success of the initiative has led IBM to publish 30,000
individual blogs (all browsable through a single location, Blog Central),
300,000 bookmarks for internal and external resources, 900 registered
communities, 10,000 activities (IBM, 2007). A similar strategy has been
implemented by Intel, with the goal of transforming "collaboration across
Intel, addressing top business challenges such as helping employees to find
relevant information and expertise more quickly, breaking down silos; attracting and retaining new employees; and capturing the tacit knowledge
of mature employees" (Intel, 2009).

However, from our survey results, SM is not being extensively implemented to benefit KM, with only 12% of respondents declaring they use
SM as an internal KM tool, and only one respondent identified that they
used internal social media "to allow knowledge flow between the entities

of the company". A simple search of Google will identify a comparative lack of articles relating to KM strategies for SM by comparison to the many SM marketing strategies, leading us to restate that KM practitioners seem to be less actively engaged.

So, in the face of this apparent lack of evangelism for SM from the KM community, one has to ask why this might be. Could it be that the KM community lacks the imagination and flexibility to see the potential of SM applications outside of their stated purpose? Whilst there is significant evidence as to how SM can be used to generate brand awareness and customer centric feedback, these tools were not designed specifically with those purposes in mind. Facebook was born as a social network to allow people to stay in touch with friends and family. However, the use of it as a marketing tool is turning out to be popular, whereas the KM potential which it has in terms of knowledge sharing and creation is being apparently unexploited or at least unrecognised.

Wikis, social network aggregation and social bookmarking tools are capable and effective in the management of unstructured data and, with their collaborative nature, have capacity for consolidating disparate insight. It seems most surprising that of the survey's respondents, they are used by only 46%, 10% and 24% respectively. Could it be that the concept of folksonomies and the unstructured tagging of items, practices closely associated with and essential to the effectiveness of these applications, may perhaps run counter to some strongly held views of those coming from a more structured information management background? In the area of ideagoras and crowd-sourcing opportunities, only 16% of companies declare they use SM for crowd sourcing, however 30% said they are using SM for Co-Creation and broadly speaking 30% of respondents are using or intend to use an idea repository. This must be encouraging, but a closer examination of the application of these techniques appears to show that the ambition in this department may be somewhat limited or not well understood.

SM has, along with much of the online world, a tremendous democratising power with its strengths being based upon popular, common and simple participation. The agenda is predominately set by the participants and much of its power comes from the emergent qualities of this approach.

Insight mined from this can often be regarded as more "truthful" and consequently as a method of gaining customer perceptions it offers a very compelling proposition to marketers. This is despite the fact that in many ways this methodology runs counter to much traditional thinking in marketing which has focused on building and controlling messages from the centre. This is becoming increasingly difficult to do as the SM tools lead to an explosive mix of multiple publishers in multiple channels and media, making it all but impossible to control or manage "the message". Despite the need for marketers to rethink some strongly held views in order to thrive in this environment, they do seem to be adapting more readily to the opportunities on offer. In the KM domain, this emergent and broad participation at the heart of SM has, to our mind, equal if not more potential. The ability to harness distributed cognition and contextually sensitive access to resources is all but unprecedented. By that we mean it is the practitioners themselves in the field that best decide on the application and value of resources, not the KM team, but this begins to take us towards a broader definition of KM and its scope than the more traditional interpretation of the discipline.

Perhaps marketing and communications communities have developed more compelling business cases that allow them to champion the use of SM effectively to senior management. After all, there are many apocryphal stories of both visible success in the use of SM from a marketing perspective, and disasters from a Marcomms perspective resulting from a lack of effective engagement with SM. These stories, true or not, can gather a momentum that can be useful in making the case for engagement. Perhaps marketers have simply become comfortable in the role as owners of the SM space. The Social Media Today website (Social Media Today, 2010) unapologetically describes itself as "The Web's Best Thinkers on Social Media and Web 2.0" and "The Moderated Business Community for Marketers, PR and Media Professionals."

Could it be that a narrow interpretation of what constitutes the function of KM makes it more problematic to make a strong argument to exploit SM for KM ends? If we take KM from a relatively narrow perspective of being focused on information management, the application of SM could appear more limited. However, if we took a broader perspective of KM as a more holistic discipline, it is reasonable to incorporate networking, customer insight, community involvement, crowd sourcing and even hiring or talent management as part of a KM brief. If we were to use this wider definition, the survey results would imply that KM is the primary application of SM, it is just that few see it that way. Could it be then that the KM community itself that has ceded the role as major evangelists for SM by constraining the view of what is within their domain?

An additional reason why Knowledge Managers are apparently not taking the lead could be that SM is transforming the KM paradigm. As Suarez states (IBM, 2007), "SM is more successful at achieving the same ends of KM, regarding explicit knowledge which is codified and stored as Intellectual Capital. There's always been less attention regarding tacit knowledge, certainly less solutions to how it can be effectively captured (if it can be). SM aims to enable instant access to relevant codified knowledge and expertise, due to its searchability and the nature of tagging."

The requirement to amass and manage knowledge seen as Intellectual Capital is now being challenged by a "social action" which arises spontaneously as an activity of daily work and, as our survey's results seem to suggest, also of daily life outside work, driven by natural motivations, i.e. sharing what one knows, whenever they want to and in whatever form, without any artificial process and fitting abstractions. We all become knowledge managers somehow, the end users are in control of information, which is structured dynamically based on subject tags that arise from shared usage. This might frighten the KM community as they feel threatened in their leading position as managers of knowledge.

5   Conclusions

Whilst it is apparent that SM is taking a firmer hold in business, its use is wider, less constrained and has been active for longer than we had expected. It is also apparent that the KM community is not leading, or perceived to be leading, the adoption of SM. This seems to us to be a missed opportunity. SM could and should be returning business value to organisations in a KM context and whilst it is not seen to be doing so, there must be risks that the best advantage of SM may not be being won. Whilst the survey does not offer any definitive answers to explain why it is that KM seems so underrepresented in this area, it must warrant further investigation. Reasons for the findings may include the following; that the KM community is not convinced of SM's value (or that the risks of its use outweigh its advantages); that they are unable to make a compelling business case to influence decision makers to adopt (unlike apparently the Marketers can); KM feels the application of SM is in areas that they perceive to be outside of the their domain. The perception of users of SM and respondents to the survey is that the application of SM is outside of their understanding of what constitutes KM.

Whatever the reasons, it seems KM is not tweeting.

References

AIIM (2010) AIIM – Find, Control and Optimize Your Information [online], AIIM, http://www.aiim.org

Dysart, J. (2008), "IFLA: Monitoring the Pulse of KM", Information Today. Medford. Vol. 25, No. 9, October 2008, p. 32 (1 pp.)

Firestone, J (2009), "Debunking conjecture of KM v. SM cultural war", Inside Knowledge, Vol. 12, No. 15

Goad, R. (2009) Hitwise Intelligence – Robin Goad – UK [online]. Experian, http://weblogs.hitwise.com/robin-goad/2009/01/twitter_traffic_up_10-fold.html

IBM (2007) Getting into social software...take the experience of IBM [online], IBM, http://www-01.ibm.com/software/lotus/news/social_software.html

Kaplan, A.M., Haenlein, M. (2010) "Users of the world, unite! The challenges and opportunities of Social Media", Business Horizons, Vol. 53, No. 1, January-February, pp. 59-68

Intel (2009) Developing an Enterprise Social Computer Strategy [online], Intel, http://download.intel.com/it/pdf/Developing_an_Enterprise_Social_Computing_strategy.pdf

Journalism.co.uk (2010) Survey: small businesses don't have time to use social media to generate new business [online], Journalism.co.uk, http://www.journalism.co.uk/66/articles/538025.php

Levy, M. (2009) "WEB 2.0 implications on knowledge management", Journal of Knowledge Management, Vol. 13, No. 1, pp 120-134

Li, C., Bernoff, J. (2008) "Groundswell: Winning in a World Transformed by Social Technologies", Harvard Business School Press

Mancini, John (2010) 30% use Twitter for BUSINESS networking at least once per day... [online], Digital Landfill, http://aiim.typepad.com/aiim_blog/2010/02/30-use-twitter-for-business-networking-at-least-once-per-day.html

McNairn, I. (2009), Using Social Software to Market yourself - inside and outside the firewall [online], SlideShow, http://www.slideshare.net/IanSMcN/using-social-software-to-market-yourself-inside-and-outside-the-firewall

Pro Inno Europe (2009) PRO INNNO Europe® [online], Pro Inno Europe, http://www.proinno-europe.eu/metrics

Review Paper (2009) "Making the most of web 2.0 technologies", Strategic Direction, Vol. 25, No. 8, pp 20–23.

Social Media Today (2010) Social Media Today | A business community for the web's best thinkers on social Media, Social Media Today, http://www.socialmediatoday.com

Tapscot, D., Williams, A. (2007) "Wikinomics: How Mass Collaboration Changes Everything", Published Atlantic Books 2007UK IPO (2009) IP Healthcheck Series – Confidential Disclosure Agreements [online], UK IPO, http://www.ipo.gov.uk/cda.pdf

Knowledge Conversion and Social Networks in Driving Team Performance

Minna Janhonen[1] and Jan-Erik Johanson[2]

[1]Finnish Institute of Occupational Health, Work and Society Team, Helsinki, Finland

[2]University of Helsinki, Department of Political and Economic Studies, Finland

Originally published in the Proceedings of ECKM 2010

Editor's Commentary

This paper looks at how different KM processes based on Nonaka's SECI model and social networking affect team performance. The authors investigate four interesting hypotheses. One interesting result was that while team members saw the three SECI conversion types: socialization, internalization and combination as valuable, senior management only saw socialization as valuable. One not too surprising result, to me at least, was that lively team interaction was one of the keys to performance. This is what socialization is all about – the everyday conversations and interactions in which people engage with each other. I often go as far to say that the aim of Knowledge Management should be enabling better conversations.

Abstract: This study aims to find out how different processes of knowledge management and patterns of social networking affect team performance. Our data on teams originate from a sample of different organizations from a variety of both public and private industries in Finland (76 teams; 499 employees). Our aim was to put the team phenomenon into an everyday context by analysing the interplay of knowledge creation and social networks in teams which function on a permanent basis. Both knowledge creation and social networking proved to be drivers of performance, but the results showed that whereas team members see the knowledge conversion processes as central to performance, top management emphasize the importance of social networks in value creation. In our examination, lively within-team interaction combined with leaders' access to the host organization was found to be the key to team performance.

Keywords: Knowledge management, social networks, teams, teamwork, performance

1 Introduction

Knowledge and social networks play an ever increasing role in creating the performance of 21st century organizations. Knowledge creation provides an organization with an intangible resource that enhances its ability to adapt to a changing environment (e.g. Nonaka et al. 2006). It is difficult to duplicate (Coakes et al. 2008). The essence of knowledge creation and management is especially important in team-based organizations (e.g. Kirkman & Shapiro, 2001; Ancona & Bressman, 2007). Teams must integrate, synthesize, and share information throughout a performance episode (Salas et al., 2008).

Our aim is to put the team phenomenon into an everyday context by analysing the interplay of knowledge creation and social networks in the performance of teams which function on a permanent basis. This study addresses to some of the inadequacies identified by previous team research. The social network analysis employed in this study enables assessment of interdependence among team members as well as their contacts to the host organization. Teams studied here originate from a sample of different organizations from a variety of industries, both public and private.

First, the theories concerning knowledge management and networking in team settings are introduced. Then we describe the study setting and methodology. In the empirical part of our inquiry we contrast the knowledge-based and network-based explanations of team performance. We included performance indices evaluated by both team members and the top management of the organizations (see Delarue et al. 2008 for a review). In the concluding section, we assess the findings in relation to the practical developments of organizing work, as well as in the theoretical context of knowledge creation and networks.

2   Processes of knowledge creation

Organizational knowledge creation is defined by Nonaka et al. (2006, p. 1179) as "the process of making available and amplifying knowledge created by individuals as well as crystallizing and connecting with an organizations' knowledge system. In this sense, knowledge creation and codification is an important part of a firm's strategy". However, knowledge creation and codification processes do not necessarily lead to performance improvement. (Alavi & Leidner, 2001): value is created only when knowledge is shared throughout an organization and applied exactly where it is needed. Therefore, firms' competitive advantages depend not only on knowledge creation but more importantly on knowledge diffusion and application (e.g. Grant, 1996), which takes place in social interaction among organizational units (Tsai & Ghosal, 1998; Nahapiet & Ghosal, 1998)

Our theoretical view on knowledge is based on organizational knowledge-creation theory (KCT), which aims to point out the dynamism of knowledge production by examining knowledge creation through the interaction of its explicit and tacit elements (Nonaka 1991). By doing this, KCT aims at complementing the static view of "knowledge assets" utilized by former theories of the knowledge-based view (e.g. Grant, 1996), and the theory of dynamic capabilities (e.g. Teece et al. 1997).

In the knowledge-creation theory, tacit and explicit knowledge are 'mutually complementary' in that they dynamically interact with each other in creative activities by individuals and groups. Knowledge that can be uttered, formulated in sentences, and captured in drawings is explicit. It is universal and accessible through consciousness. Knowledge tied to the senses, tactile experiences, movement skills, intuition, unarticulated mental models, or implicit rules of thumb, is tacit. Tacit knowledge is rooted in action, procedures, routines, commitment, ideals, values, and emotions. The concept of 'knowledge conversion' explains how tacit and explicit knowledge interact along the continuum. The conversion occurs in four processes: socialization, externalization, combination and internalization (the SECI model). (Nonaka 1991; Nonaka & Takeuchi, 1994.)

Socialization (tacit to tacit) facilitates the exchange of tacit knowledge via joint activities in social interaction. For a workgroup, tacit knowledge-sharing among members is critical for task completion and performance. In the socio-psychological tradition, socialization has been seen as process which helps people successfully adjust to the organization (Louis, 1980, 229-230).

The process of Externalization (tacit to explicit) includes the translation of tacit knowledge into comprehensible forms that can be understood by others. This process can be supported by two the articulation of tacit knowledge transfers the "invisible" ideas and images into "visual" forms, and by translating the tacit knowledge of different interest groups, like customers and experts, into understandable forms. In the group context, this is partly the work that crosses group boundaries.

Combination (explicit to explicit) involves the amalgamation of existing data and information to create more shareable forms, and the integration of explicit knowledge into the firm's knowledge base, via the IT systems. Johannessen et al. (2001) sees that placing too much importance on the idea that knowledge can be properly transferred through IT channels may even relegate the importance of tacit knowledge as an important strategic resource for most companies.

Internalization (explicit to tacit) is analogous to 'learning by doing'. It generates fresh tacit knowledge, thus renewing the spiral. People talk and think about the explicit knowledge embodied in documents, manuals, computer systems etc; gain experience, recognize gaps in their know-how; and broaden, extend and reframe their tacit knowledge.

If all the phases of knowledge management are utilized well, the knowledge management spiral is balanced (e.g. Nonaka & von Krogh, 2009). In line of this argument, Johannessen et al. (2001) says that the entire knowledge base has to be emphasized if a firm wishes to gain a competitive advantage both internally and externally. Over-emphasizing either explicit of tacit knowledge, may lead to a situation in which companies lose their competitive edge. Current research has found support for these arguments (e.g. Blumenberg, Wagner & Beimborn, 2009). This allows us to formulate our first hypothesis:

Hypothesis 1: Knowledge conversion promotes team performance

The use of tacit and explicit knowledge can be balanced to positively impact the outcome of a company when practitioners learn to identify and remove obstacles to knowledge conversion, such as a lack of resources (Blumenberg et al., 2009). Removing these obstacles is especially important because knowledge transfer and the development of shared knowledge influence organizational performance.

3 Team social networks

The knowledge creation and social networks within teams are two sides of the same coin. In a sense, social networks are conduits by which information and knowledge proceeds in an organizational setting.

When teams face new challenges, members should critically examine and question their competencies and resources for producing the desired output. The question is remarkably important in so-called permanent work teams, which are not invented for carrying out a particular task, but more a method of organizing inside the firm. Internal operations are not enough to keep teams alive, and the desired output is best achieved through the integration of the team's internal and external contacts (Hoegl, Parboteeah & Munson, 2003).

So far, there is not much evidence on the performance outcomes of specific network structures within an organizational context (Flap et al., 1998). Moreover, most of the empirical results come from innovation teams performing non-standard duties. The existence of core periphery structures, i.e. a separation into a strongly connected core and a weakly connected periphery within teams, decreased the performance as evaluated by the leaders (Cummings & Cross, 2003). On the other hand, network density has been shown both to increase productivity (Reagans & Zuckerman, 2001) and to decrease creative performance (Kratzer et al. 2004).

Numerous studies have shown the advantages of the successful integration of knowledge across team and organizational boundaries, and provide specific examples from a real-world context for the hypothesized possibility of integrating knowledge externally (Grant, 1996; Tsai & Ghosal, 1998; Hoegl. et al. 2003; Ancona & Bresman, 2007). Networks that allow knowledge transfer among teams provide opportunities for learning and co-operation, at the same time enabling the creation of new knowledge and enhancing the organization's ability to innovate (Tsai & Ghosal, 1998). According to Hoegl et al. (2003), the growth of individuals' knowledge networks will generally ease the task of knowledge generation and dissemination throughout an organization, by widening existing communication channels.

What kinds of network structures enhance knowledge-sharing? Blumenberg et al. (2009) suggest that tacit knowledge can be successfully shared if the frequency of interaction and closeness is high. This kind of knowledge transfer leads to increased shared knowledge that in turn may affect performance. Several other studies have come to similar conclusions. Different studies (e.g. Mehra et al., 2001; Balkundi & Harrison, 2006) point out that the density and resourcefulness of an individual's informal personal contacts (i.e. his/her knowledge network) are essential for the 'team spirit' or 'teamness' of the team, but also important to both individual and team performance. This makes us argue that:

Hypothesis 2: Lively interaction within the team increases performance

Not all networks are desirable however. The development and maintenance of contacts can be time-consuming and may divert attention from performing productive activities, or undermine group cohesion (Alderfer, 1977; Ancona & Bressman, 2007). Furthermore, it is possible that not everyone should be networking. It may be preferable, for example, to have "gatekeepers" do all the networking instead of every team member being engaged in it (Hoegl, Parboteeah & Munson, 2003).

Some studies have argued that team leaders' networks are more important than team members' contacts, because leaders' contacts are usually directed at more valuable sources. Brass et al. (2004) argue that these leaders' contacts can gain performance advantages. On the other hand, a person's position in an organizational hierarchy doesn't necessarily reveal much about the knowledge he/she possesses (Ancona & Bresman, 2007). In theory, teams are designed for equal knowledge-sharing, not for leader-domination of knowledge. However, in practice, leaders can still be gatekeepers of the knowledge flow (Kilduff & Tsai, 2003). This makes us assume that both team leaders' and team members' social networks outside the team can be useful for knowledge-sharing.

Hypothesis 3a: Team members' external relationships contribute to team performance.

Hypothesis 3b: Team leaders' external relationships contribute to team performance.

Johannessen et al. (2001) point out the importance of balanced (both tacit and explicit) knowledge-sharing, and show the importance of both internal and external social networks in this process. According to the importance of social networks from the knowledge conversion perspective, we assume that the balance of the team social network structure, by which we mean both the internally dense (as proposed for example by Blumenberg et al. 2009 and Mehra et al. 2001) and the externally actively networked structure (as proposed for example by Hoegl et al., 2003 and Nonaka & von Krogh, 2009), has a positive effect on team performance. This leads us to argue:

Hypothesis 4: Both team internal and external social networks contribute to team performance

4 Methods and measures

The data of the study consists of 499 employees in 76 teams, which were situated in 49 work organizations. Of the teams, 42 operated in the public sector and 34 in the private sector. Team size varied from 3 to 15 members, which is seen as "normal" team size (Mueller et al., 2000). Teams in which less than 80% of the members had completed the questionnaire were excluded from the analysis, as the network analytic approach is vulnerable to missing values (Wasserman & Faust, 1994). All the teams included in the study were permanent work teams. The means and standard deviations of the independent variables are shown in Table 1 (see Appendix).

4.1 Dependent variables

Team performance

Team performance was evaluated using two measurements: first, according to the team members' and leader's own evaluations of their team's abilities, and second, according to the organization's top management's (HR manager or executive) evaluation.

The measurement of the team members' own evaluation of their team's performance was made according to three items: the team works effectively; the team works fluently; the team works better than other teams (semantic differentials; scale 1-7; Cronbach's alpha =.82)

The top management's evaluation consisted of two items: team overall performance (4-10); and team quality (moderately performing or well-performing). The items were scaled so that the grade of overall performance was multiplied by 0.5 when team quality was evaluated as moderate, and by 1.5 when it was evaluated as good (scale 3.5 - 13.5).

4.2 Independent variables

The four knowledge conversion processes in teams were measured using Bennett's (2001) operationalization of Nonaka-Takeutchi's (1995) tacit and explicit model, which was adapted to the team-level. Internalization was measured using four arguments concerning the guidelines of information flow and knowledge-sharing within the team (scale 1-5; mean 3.54; std. 0.76; Cronbach's alpha =0.59). Socialization was measured using four items concerning joint team activities (scale 1-5; mean 3.75; std. 0.81; Cronbach's alpha =0.67). Externalization was measured using two items concerning co-operation guidelines between teams (scale 1-5; mean 3.73; std. 0.88; Cronbach's alpha = 0.59). Combination was measured using four items regarding the integration of explicit knowledge into teams' knowledge bases (scale 1-5; mean 3.13; std. 0.92; Cronbach's alpha = 0.68). The items were measured using a five-point Likert scale (1 = fully disagree, 5 = fully agree).

Network measures

Internal networks: In the analysis of lively team interaction, the questionnaire was customized according to the respondent, so that the names of individual team members were included in the questionnaire. For measuring the communication network, the following question was formulated "Who do you communicate with, and how often?". Respondents were requested to mark all relevant members of the team. The derived network measures used in the data analysis were based on density measures

(Wasserman & Faust, 1994). Density refers to the number of actual contacts in relation to the theoretical maximum. In this study, density varied from 0.00 to 1.00, meaning that 0%, and 100% respectively of all possible relationships between team members were present. External networks: These analyses are performed according to so-called ego-network methodology (Wasserman & Faust, 1994). In our study we examined only the positions of the alters (top management, middle management, experts, other work groups, other employees, administration). The frequency of the contacts was elicited and measured as strength of the relationship (daily = 4, weekly = 3, monthly = 2, few times a year = 1, not at all = 0). The frequency of the connections was summed at personal level to describe overall external activity (scale 0-24). We similarly enquired about team members' and leaders' external connections to inter-organizational actors and their strength. The frequency of inter-organizational connections varied from 0 (not at all) to 4 (daily).

4.3　Control variables

The size of teams included in this study varied from 3 to 15 members (mean 8.74; sd. 3.48). The sectoral alignment was a dummy variable, with the public sector as a reference category.

Table 1 (appendix) shows the means, standard deviations, and correlations of independent variables. As regards the linear regression models presented in Tables 2 and 3 (appendix), the values of variance inflation factors (VIFs) associated with each of the independent variables are within a range of 1.108 to 3.026 (mean 1,77). Thus the effects of multicollinearity are within acceptable limits (Hair et al., 1998).

Linear regression analysis was used for examining the relationships between the dependent and independent factors. We first studied the direct effect between team performance and processes of knowledge management (Step 1). Next, the measurements concerning social networks were included into the model (Step 2). In step 3, both knowledge conversion and social network variables were added. Finally, in step 4, the effect of team size and sectoral alignment (public vs. private) were controlled for in the models.

5 Results

Tables 2 and 3 (see appendix) show the regression analyses results of the effects of knowledge conversion and team social network structure on team performance. In the first step of the analysis, when the relationship between KM processes and Team members' performance evaluation (Table 2) was examined, we found a positive relationship to internalization, socialization and combination. In step 2, we saw that although the density of the internal team communication network and the contacts of both team members, as well as that of the team leader to the host organization, are beneficial for performance, but team leaders' inter-organizational contacts are actually detrimental to performance. In step 3, we looked at the relationship between the team social network and team members' performance evaluation together with processes of knowledge conversion. The effect of networks varies: the network density and team members' intra-organization network were not related to team effectiveness in this model. In step 4, the analysis showed that small team size is beneficial for team performance, and the positive effect of network density and that the negative effect of team members' inter-organizational networks also appear. The situation is different in regard to the top managers' performance evaluation (Table 3). From the processes of knowledge conversion, only socialization is related to top managers' performance evaluation in the first step. The application of team social network to the model (step 2) indicates that density of communication network and team leader's intra-organizational social network promotes performance, whereas inter-organizational network decreases it. Inclusion of both knowledge management and social network variables provides little change (step 3). Small team size advances team performance and sector has no effect.

The results provide partial support for hypothesis 1. Knowledge conversion processes other than externalization are important in team members' evaluations of performance, and the significance of socialization is prominent in top management evaluations. Hypothesis 2 related to the beneficial influence of lively interaction within the team, and received support in both evaluations. While hypothesis 3a, related to the external contacts of team members, was not supported and hypothesis 3b, was partially supported: leaders' contacts to the host organization received strong support irrespective of the evaluator. Furthermore, leader's inter-organizational contacts seem to be detrimental for team performance. The argument of hypothesis 4; that both team internal and external social networks contribute to team performance, is supported in both evaluations, although the fruitfulness of these interactions is hierarchically ordered and organization-based.

6 Discussion and conclusions

The study aimed at analysing the significance of knowledge creation processes and social networking for the performance of ordinary teams performing their duties on a permanent basis. Both knowledge creation processes and social networks defined the performance of the team. In our study, both team members as well as the top management assessed the performance of the teams which revealed significant divergences in drivers of performance. Team members emphasized knowledge conversion and top management social networking. Members saw many types of knowledge conversion resulting in performance (socialization, internalization, and combination), but top management only saw socialization practices as beneficial for performance. Echoing earlier findings, it might be that unity in itself is valued property of performance in management evaluations. From the bird's eye perspective of the top management, the patterns of social intercourse among team members might be an approximate measure of knowledge creation, whereas from the shop floor perspective of the team members, success originates from a variety of knowledge creation and networking processes.

The fact that our sample of teams consisted of ordinary teams dealing with standard duties might have had an influence on the results. Our focus was on relationships beneficial for performance and not the existence of external relationships as such. In this sense, the hierarchical ordering of relationships proved to be a key success factor of the team. This is not an image of a boundaryless organization (Ashkenas et al. 1995) but rather an extension of a hierarchy in a team-based context which could be called "teamarchy". The most important feature of teamarchy in contrast to traditional hierarchies is the importance of the lively interaction within teams. These results make us argue that performance in this kind of team mostly depends on team socialization (i.e. gaining the functional skills or abilities required, getting along with organizational culture, supporting and being supported by peers, and having a feeling of self-fulfilment), which takes place in dense intra-team communication networks.

Our examination points to a selective balance between knowledge creation and social networks (e.g. Johannessen, 2001). Knowledge creation internal to the team is important, but external contacts serve purposes other than disseminating knowledge for the use of others. As even the most work-related networks might function as conduits channelling a variety of instrumental and emotional resources, it is likely that the role of the team leader's external contacts to host organizations in supporting performance are based on other aspects of networking, such as diverting resources for the use of the focal team. Another feature of the balance is the information processing capacity of employees. Too much emphasis on external contacts puts team identity at risk, and also endangers team identity (Choi 2002).

Our study has some practical implications. The importance of teams as social contexts provides a strong platform for socialization and co-worker support, but local social intercourse also easily results in local social identities. The significance of lively interaction between the team and the host organization cannot be assessed solely on the basis of performance. To make strong team players into good citizens of the organisation, team members will be required to form external links that are irrelevant or detrimental for performance, but which provide a sense of togetherness in the organizational arena.

7 Limitations

Earlier empirical and theoretical work has shown that knowledge creation cannot be separated from the context in which it is created. Our data originated from a variety of teams in a single country, which enabled us to include a variety of industries in our analysis, but at the same time it deprived us of the option to compare other national contexts. We encourage the examination of ordinary teams performing standard duties in other national contexts to validate our findings.

8 Acknowledgements

The Finnish Work Environment Fund and Academy of Finland have supported this study

References

Alavi, M. and Leidner. D.E. (2001) "Knowledge management and knowledge management systems: Conceptual foundations and research issues", MIS Quaterly, Vol 25, pp 107–136.

Alderfer, C.P. (1977) Group and intergroup relations. In Hackman, J.R. & Suttle, J.L. (eds.): Improving the quality of work life. Goodyear, Palisades, C.A. pp. 227-296.

Ancona, D. and Bresman, H. (2007) X-teams: How to build teams that lead, innovate and succeed. Harvard Business School Press, Boston, Massachusetts.

Ashkenas R., Ulrich D., Jick T. and Kerr S. (1998) The Boundaryless Organization: Breaking the Chains of Organizational Structure. San Francisco: Jossey-Bass

Bakundi, P. and Harrison, D.A. (2006) "Ties, leaders and time in teams: Strong inference about network structure's effects on team viability and performance", Academy of Management Journal, Vol 49, pp 49-68.

Blumenberg, S., Wagner, H-T. and Beimborn, D. (2009) "Knowledge transfer processes in IT outsourcing relationships and their impact on shared knowledge and outsourcing performance", International Journal of Information Management, Vol 29, pp 342-352.

Brass D. J., Galaskiewicz, J., Greve H. R. and Tsai W. (2004) "Taking stock of networks and organizations: a multilevel perspective", Academy of Management Journal, Vol 47,pp 795–817.

Choi, J.N. (2002) "External activities and team effectiveness: review and theoretical development", Small Group Research, Vol 33,pp 181-208.

Coakes, E.W., Coakes, J.M. and Rosenberg, D. (2008) "Co-operative work practices and knowledge sharing issues: A comparison of viewpoints", International Journal of Information Management, Vol 28, pp 12-25.

Cohen, S.G.. and Bailey, D.E. (1997) "What makes teams work: Group effectiveness research from the shop floor to the executive suite", Journal of Management, Vol 23, pp 239-290.

Cummings J. and Cross, R. (2003) "Structural properties of work groups and their consequences for performance", Social Networks, Vol 25, pp 197-210.

Delarue, A., Hootegem, G. Van, Procter, S. and Burridge, M. (2008) "Teamworking and organizational performance: A review of survey-based research", International Journal of Management Reviews, Vol 10, pp 127-148.

Flap, H., Bulder, B., and Volker, B. (1998) "Intra-organisational networks and performance: a review", Computational & Mathematical Organization Theory, Vol 4, pp 109-147.

Grant, R. (1996) "Toward a knowledge-based theory of the firm", Strategic Management Journal, Vol. 17(Winter), pp 109–122.

Guzzo, R.A. and Dickson, M.W. (1996) "Teams in organizations: Recent research on performance and effectiveness", Annual Review of Psychology, Vol 47, pp 307-338.

Hair, J.F.jr., Anderson, R.E., Tatham, R.C., and Black, W.C. (1998) Multivariate data analysis. Upper Saddle River, NJ: Prentice-Hall.

Hoegl, M., Parboteeah, P. and Munson, C.L. (2003) "Team-level antecedents of individuals' knowledge networks", Decision Sciences, Vol 34, pp 741-770.

Johannessen, J-A., Olaisen, J. and Olsen, B. (2001) "Mismanagement of tacit knowledge: the importance of tacit knowledge, the danger of information technology, and what to do about it", International Journal of Information Management, Vol 21, pp 3-20.

Kilduff, M. and Tsai, W. (2003) Social Networks and Organizations. Sage Publications: London, Thousand Oaks, New Delhi.

Kirkman, B.L and Shapiro, D.L. (2001) "The impact of cultural values on job satisfaction and organizational commitment in self-managing work teams: The mediating role of employee resistance", Academy of Management Journal, Vol 44, pp 557-569.

Kratzer, J., Leenders Th. A.J. and van Engelen, J. M. (2004) "Stimulating the potential: Creative performance and communication in innovation teams",Creativity and Innovation Management, Vol 13, pp 63-71.

Louis, M.R. (1980) "Surprise and sense making: what newcomers experience in entering unfamiliar organizational settings", Administrative Science Quarterly, Vol 25, pp 226-51.

Mehra A., Kilduff M. and Brass D. J. (2001) "The social networks of high and low self-monitors: Implications for workplace performance", Administrative Science Quarterly, Vol. 46, pp 121–146.

Mueller, F., Procter, S. and Buchanan, D. (2000) "Teamworking in its context(s): Antecedents, nature and dimensions", Human Relations, Vol 53, pp 1387-1424.

Nahapiet, J. and Ghoshal, S. (1998) "Social Capital, intellectual capital, and the organizational advantage" Academy of Managemet Review, Vol 23, pp 242-266.

Nonaka, I. (1991) The knowledge-creating company. Harvard Business.Review,Vol 69, pp 96–104.

Nonaka, I. and von Krogh, G. (2009) "Tacit knowledge and knowledge conversion: controversy and advancement in organizational knowledge creation theory", Organization Science, Vol 20, pp 635-652.

Nonaka, I., von Krogh, G. and Voelpel, S. (2006) "Organizational knowledge creation theory: Evolutionary paths and future advances", Organization Studies, Vol 27, pp 1179–1208.

Nonaka, I. and Takeuchi, H. (1995) The knowledge creating company. Oxford University Press, New York, N.Y.

Reagans, R. and Zuckerman, E. (2001) "Networks, diversity, and productivity: The social capital of corporate R&D teams", Organization Science, Vol 12, pp 502-517.

Salas, E., Cooke, N.J. and Rosen, M.A. (2008) "On teams, teamwork, and team performance: discoveries and developments", Human factors, Vol 50, pp 540-547.

Stock, R. (2004) "Drivers to teamn performance: What do we know and what have we still to learn?", Schmalenbach Business Review, Vol 56, pp 274-306.

Teece, D. J., Pisano, G. and Shuen, A. (1997) "Dynamic capabilities and strategic management", Strategic Management Journal, Vol 18, pp 509–533.

Tsai,W. and Ghosal, S. (1998) "Social capital and value creation: the role of intrafirm networks", Academy of Management Journal, Vol 41, pp 464-476.

Wasserman, S. and Faust, K. (1994) Social network analysis: Methods and application. Cambridge University Press, New York.

Appendix

Table 1: Means, standard deviations and correlations of the independent variables

	mean	sd.	1.	2	3	4	5	6	7	8	9	10
1. Internalization	3.54	.761	-									
2. Socialization	3.75	.811	.560**	-								
3. Combination	3.13	.919	.327*	.396**	-							
4. Externalization	3.73	.884	.638**	.424**	.168**	-						
5. Team network density	.29	.267	.095*	.111*	-.057	.125**	-					
6. Team members' intra-Organizational networks	12.14	4.675	.272*	.306*	.309*	.241*	.042	-				
7. Team leaders' intra-organizational networks	15.07	3.924	.106*	.232*	.390*	-.043	.145*	.316*	-			
8. Team members' inter-organizational networks	1.72	1.230	.086	.146*	.185*	.070	.136*	.470*	.218*	-		
9. Team leaders' inter-organizational networks	2.36	1.234	-.006	-.087	.040	-.077	.101*	.135*	.493*	.263*	-	
10. Team size	8.74	3.488	.079	-.102*	.074	-.009	.356*	.002	.175*	.146*	.458*	
11. Sector	.46	.499	.029	-.016	.090*	-.021	-.258*	.133*	.075	.084	-.073	.013

Table 2: Regression results with team members' performance evaluation as dependent variable

	Step 1 Knowledge management	Step 2 Social networking	Step 3 Knowledge management	Step 4 Control variables

			and social networking	included
Constant	2.158** (.361)	3.833**(0,253)	2.421** (.359)	2.150** (.374)
1. Internalization	.277** (.091)		.303** (.102)	.258* (.103)
2. Socialization	.445** (.072)		.267** (.083)	.294** (.084)
3. Combination	.241** (.058)		.220** (.075)	.219** (.075)
4. Externalization	-.065 (.070)		-.088 (.077)	-.100 (.076)
5. Team network density		.815** (.261)	.317 (.275)	.694* (.317)
6. Team members' intra-organizational networks		.047**(.013)	.004 (.014)	.004 (.015)
7. Team leaders' intra-organizational networks		.086**(.017)	.057** (.018)	.051* (.018)
8. Team members' inter-organizational networks		-.081 (.046)	-.091 (.047)	-.094* (.047)
9. Team leaders' inter-organizational networks		-.192**(.049)	-.153** (.051)	-.192** (.053)
10. Team size				.048* (.021)
11. Sector				.057 (.107)
	R^2=.30 (R^2adj =.29)	R^2= .18 (R^2adj=.17)	R^2= .33 (R^2adj=.31)	R^2= .35 (R^2adj=.32)

*p<0.05, **p<0.01

Table 3: Regression results with top managers' performance evaluation as dependent variable

	Step 1 Knowledge management	Step 2 Social networking	Step 3 Knowledge management and social networking	Step 4 Control variables included
Constant	4.031** (1.154)	3,401**(.978)	3.552* (1.447)	4.585**(1.502)
1. Internalization	-.438 (.390)		-.488 (.417)	-.225 (.418)
2. Socialization	1.460** (.307)		.878** (.337)	.768* (.335)
3. Combination	.445 (.250)		.157 (.307)	.090 (.305)
4. Externalization	-.337 (.297)		-.414 (.313)	-.366 (.308)
5. Team network density		7.230 ** (1.008)	6.672** (1.111)	4.871** (1.284)
6. Team members' intra-organizational networks		-.058 (.051)	-.094 (.059)	-.113 (.058)
7. Team leaders' intra-organizational networks		.373**(.064)	.391** (.074)	.441** (.074)
8. Team members' inter-organizational networks		-.072 (0.180)	-.017 (.194)	-.025 (.192)
9. Team leaders' inter-organizational networks		-.884** (.188)	-1.052** (.204)	-.830** (.213)
10. Team size				-.244** (.084)
11. Sector				.550 (.433)
	R^2=.08 (R^2adj =.07)	R^2= .24 (R^2adj=.23)	R^2= .30 (R^2adj=.27)	R^2= .32 (R^2adj=.29)

*p<0.05, **p<0.01;

Social Capital, Knowledge Sharing and Intellectual Capital in the Web 2.0 Enabled World

Marguerite Cronk
Harding University, Searcy, Arkansas, USA
Originally published in the Proceedings of ECKM 2011

Editor's Commentary

This paper explores the relationship between social capital, knowledge sharing and intellectual capital in a Web 2.0 enabled environment. Knowledge sharing through interpersonal relationships is seen as a pivotal concept in this respect. Two key points stand out for me, that are frequently missed in discussions on Social KM. The first is that online interaction can increase most forms of social capital not diminish it. And second, Web 2.0 provides not only a platform to share but one that stimulates motivation for knowledge sharing through the development of relationships and social capital. It is this motivation that is so important if KM is to be more successful than it has been to date.

Abstract: Web 2.0 technologies have facilitated an unprecedented era of social knowledge sharing. Many businesses are examining how they can tap into this phenomenon to enhance knowledge sharing within the organization. This study explores links between social capital created through online social network knowledge sharing and Intellectual capital. It is suggested that within the organizational context, intellectual capital can be generated from social capital through knowledge sharing, facilitated by Web 2.0 technologies. The benefits of Web 2.0 technologies in the area of knowledge sharing are well documented, however this study suggests that Web 2.0 technologies not only provide the platform to share but also the motivation to share as participants gain and benefit from increased social capital, which may in turn overcome perceptions of 'loss of personal competitive advantage' concerns associated with traditional knowledge sharing.

Social Capital, Knowledge Sharing and Intellectual Capital in the Web 2.0 Enabled World

Keywords: Knowledge sharing, Intellectual capital, Web 2.0, Social Capital, Knowledge management

1 Introduction

It is a time of unprecedented internet access and connections between individuals. There is no shortage of statistics on the exponential growth of Web 2.0 sites. The rapid increase in the number and type of Web 2.0 sites, such as wikis, online social networks, blogs, Flickr, YouTube, discussion forums, mashups, and so forth makes it almost pointless to quote usage statistics, as by the time this article is published these figures will have changed significantly. However quotes such as "The number of blog sites doubles every 150 days, approximately 150,000 new blogs are added every day, wikipedia has 217 million unique visitors every month, social networking sites such as Facebook have 175 million active users with 180 million photos uploaded each month" and so forth. (Casarez 2009) are sufficient to make the point that this is no temporary fad and hence warrants investigation.

Nie (2001), argued that Internet use detracts from face-to-face time with others, which might diminish an individual's social capital. However, this perspective has received strong criticism (Bargh & McKenna, 2004). Some researchers have claimed that online interactions may supplement or replace in-person interactions, mitigating any loss from time spent online (Wellman, Haase, Witte, & Hampton, 2001). This paper suggests that online interaction can increase most forms of social capital, including those that facilitate intellectual capital building. The body of knowledge on both social and intellectual capital is immense. The literature suggests a sound theoretical link between these two constructs and knowledge sharing. This paper intends to examine these links highlighting aspects that are of particular significance to the knowledge sharing environment provided by Web 2.0 tools.

The basic proposition of this paper is that Web 2.0 tools facilitate increased knowledge sharing by not only providing an excellent platform for exchange, combination and creation of new knowledge, but also by stimulating motivation for knowledge sharing through the development of bonding and bridging social capital. The research method used in this paper is primarily literature synthesis involving inductive interpretation of qualitative research to establish associations not previously known. The paper structure will be as follows. Firstly definitions and literature on social capital, intellectual capital and Web 2.0 technologies pertinent to the proposition will be introduced. Secondly the literature will be summarized highlighting potential relationships between the constructs and a model reflecting the nature of these relationships constructed.

2 Literature review

2.1 Definitions

2.1.1 Web 2.0.

'Web 2.0' technologies refer to the range of interoperable technologies that facilitate communication in multiple formats, information sharing and critique, social exchanges, community and collective wisdom (Casarez 2009). These include social network sites such as Facebook and Myspace, wikis, blogs, flickr, youtube, discussion forums, mashups, wikis, micro-blogging and so forth.

2.1.2 Social capital

There are many definitions of Social Capital, however most revolve around the notion of shared accumulated resources that exist across social networks. The social network can be seen as the structure or system of connections between nodes. Bourdieu and Wacquant (1992) define social capital as "the sum of the resources, actual or virtual, that accrue to an individual or a group by virtue of possessing a durable network of more or less institutionalized relationships of mutual acquaintance and recognition" (p. 14).

2.1.3 Bonding Social Capital

Bonding is horizontal, among equals within a community. Bonding capital is localized which is defined as being found among people who live in the same or adjacent communities. It is also the form of social capital associated with thick trust (Anheier and Kendall 2002). It is associated with strong ties, or strong social bonds, and is called "sociological superglue" by Putman (2000).

2.1.4   Bridging Social Capital

Bridging is said to be vertical between communities (Dolfsma and Dannreuther 2003; Narayan 2002; Narayan and Pritchett 1999) Bridging capital extends to individuals and organizations that are more removed, geographically socially or emotionally. Bridging social capital is associated with thin trust and weak ties.

2.1.5   Linking Capital

Linking capital refers to relations between individuals or groups in different social starta (Cote and Healy, 2001) or groups that have nothing in common.

2.1.6   Intellectual Capital

Nahapiet and Ghoshal (1998) define "intellectual capital" as the "knowledge and knowing capability of a social collectivity, such as an organization, intellectual community, or professional practice". Jar-Der (2005), refer to intellectual capital as the knowledge possessed by groups that is more than the aggregation of individual groups.

Each of the above defined constructs has multiple definitions and sub-components. The intention behind selecting broad definitions is to establish possible relationships between the constructs at the macro level, and suggest areas for further investigation.

2.2   Social capital and Social networks

In order to establish a context, the following section briefly defines social capital, notes benefits derived from social capital and examines social capital in the virtual space.

Social capital is a somewhat elastic term with a variety of definitions in multiple fields (Adler & Kwon, 2002), and is conceived of as both a cause and an effect (Resnick, 2001; Williams, 2006). As stated above, Bourdieu and Wacquant (1992) define social capital as "the sum of the resources, actual or virtual, that accrue to an individual or a group by virtue of possessing a durable network of more or less institutionalized relationships of mutual acquaintance and recognition" (p. 14). The resources from these relationships can differ in form and function based on the relationships themselves. Social capital broadly refers to the *resources accumulated through the relationships* or connections among people (Coleman, 1988). Some authors distinguish between various forms of social capital and others refer to it as collective term. Generally speaking social capital has been linked to a variety of positive social outcomes, such as better public health, lower crime rates, and more efficient financial markets (Adler & Kwon, 2002). Moreover, social capital researchers have found that various forms of social capital, including ties with friends and neighbors, are related to indices of psychological well-being, such as self esteem and satisfaction with life (Bargh & McKenna, 2004; Helliwell & Putnam, 2004). Vertovec (2001) highlighted the benefits of using social networks, by explaining how interpersonal relations cut across boundaries such as neighborhood, workplace, kinship or class and could be abstracted on an individual basis (Vivian and Fay 2003)

Even though most of the research on social capital focuses on the collective benefits of social capital as discussed above, Bourdieu and Coleman (1991), provide conceptualization at the individual level. They believe that social capital exists between individuals and can be studied at the individual level. Social capital is said to reside in the relations (links) among the nodes (individuals) of a network and 'just as physical and human capital facilitate productive activity, social capital does as well' (Coleman, 1988, p 101). Social capital is said to exist between individuals and by extension can be accumulated by the individuals. Such a view of social capital rests on the premise that *'my connections can help me'* (Cross and Cummings, 2004) and is all about establishing relationships purposefully and employing them to generate intangible and tangible benefits in short or long terms. Hence it is suggested that the study of individual connections may provide insight into the development of the social network and resulting social capital.

In a *virtual setting,* social capital is said to be a common social resource that facilitates information exchange, knowledge sharing, and knowledge construction through continuous interaction, built on trust and maintained through shared understanding (Daniel, Schwier & McCalls, 2003). It is assumed this refers more to the bonding social capital as bonding has more to do with trust (Nahapiet and Ghoshal (1998). Huysman and Wulf (2005), propose that the higher the level of social capital, the more members are *stimulated to connect and share knowledge*. This sharing aspect challenges individuals to *draw upon and provide value for themselves* and the community, with obvious benefits to both parties. This notion is in a way a demonstration of the purposeful establishment of relationships for mutual benefit suggested by Cummings and Cross (2004) above.

As defined above, bonding social capital is associated with strong ties. It refers to the kinds of support that originates in close knit relations such as intimate friends and family (Putnam, 2000). Bonding social capital in an organizational implies that there is trust and a sense of obligation that encourages reciprocity (Steinfield et. al, 2009). Social networking site studies have reported the usage of such sites association with increased bonding capital, for example, directed communication between friends. This may take the form of wall posts between friends intended for and consumed by a close friend (Burke et al 2010). It is suggested that the greater the degree of sharing, the greater the degree of bonding social capital within the network. In addition to strengthening already strong bonds, web based social networking strengthens weak ties as more is shared with those more distant (emotionally socially or geographically). For example, a connection may be made with an acquaintance from the distant past, country, or a friend of a friend. At the point the connection is made the tie is weak and little is known of the 'friend'. After the newly connected friend shared their thoughts, photos and experiences, a stronger understanding and emotional connection is made transforming this connection from a weak tie to stronger or possibly from bridging to bonding capital.

Both bridging and linking capital are said to be associated with notions of 'getting ahead' creating opportunities and the ability to leverage resources. Studies of social networking sites list advancement of career, support for campaigns or projects, and expectations from an extended network. (DiMicco, 2008; Morris et al,2010)

Ellison et al (2007), investigated the linkages between Facebook usage and various types of social capital and found a positive relationship between certain kinds of Facebook use and the maintenance and creation of social capital including bridging (between communities) and to a lesser extent bonding social capital (among individuals within a community). Recently, researchers have emphasized the importance of Internet-based linkages for the formation of weak ties (temporary and contingent), which serve as the foundation of bridging social capital and suggest that it is possible that new forms of social capital and relationship building such as bridging social capital will occur in online social network sites (Ellison et al., 2007).

In summary it can be said that participation in web2 social networking, increases social capital.(see figure 1.)

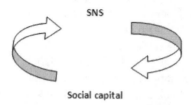

SNS

Social capital

Figure 1: Relationship between Web 2.0 Social Networking and Social Capital.

2.3 Social capital and knowledge sharing in the Web 2.0 environment

Social capital is the shared accumulated resources that exist across social networks. Knowledge is the primary resource shared and accumulated in the network. Social relations, often established for other purposes, constitute information channels that reduce the amount of time and investment required to gather information. (Nahapiet and Ghoshal 1998). As mentioned above the amount and nature of what is being shared depends on the type of social capital. For example, there is mounting evidence demonstrating that where parties trust each other, they are more willing to engage in cooperative activity through which further trust may be generated (Fukuyama, 1995; Putnam, 1993; Tyler & Kramer, 1996). Morris et al (2010) suggests that web2 social network users actually use the network to both gain and share knowledge (as information, knowledge, or experience) by asking questions as their 'status. In this study network users site speedier better quality information, as the motivator as it comes from a trusted source (group of friends).

Studies of knowledge sharing in the Web 2.0 era have ventured down some different paths than in the 'pre' Web 2.0 studies. For example, in relation to social technologies 'connectivists' assert that knowledge is distributed across a network of connections, and therefore that learning consists of the ability to construct and traverse those networks. Some domains of knowledge contain vast numbers of weak interrelations that, if properly exploited, can greatly amplify learning by a process of inference (Siemens, 2004; Downes 2006). This sounds very similar to 'accumulated shared resources' or social capital. These authors refer to learning specifically, but knowledge sharing/transfer is a precursor to learning.

Hence the significance of web2 in knowledge sharing is not only to provide an excellent sharing platform but to assist in the building of social capital which in turn fuels more knowledge sharing. (See figure 2.)

Figure 2: The relationship between Social Capital and Knowledge Sharing, facilitated by Web 2.0 SNS.

2.4   Social capital and intellectual capital

Nahapiet and Ghoshal 1998 define "intellectual capital" as the "knowledge and knowing capability of a *social* collectivity, such as an organization, intellectual community, or professional practice. They defend their definition in terms of its clear parallel with the concept of human capital, which embraces the acquired knowledge, skills, and capabilities that enable persons to act in new ways (Coleman, 1988). They affirm the notion that social capital facilitates the creation of new intellectual capital (Nahapiet and Ghoshal 1998) through knowledge processes. (See figure 3)

Figure 3: The relationship between Social Capital and Intellectual Capital, facilitated by Knowledge Sharing

2.5 Intellectual capital and knowledge sharing

Knowledge sharing appears to be the intersection or pivotal point that both social capital and intellectual capital revolve around.

Following Schumpeter (1934), Moran and Ghoshal (1996) have argued that all new resources, including knowledge, are created through two generic processes: namely, combination and exchange. There appears to be a consensus that both types of knowledge creation involve making new combinations either by combining elements previously unconnected or by developing novel ways of combining elements previously associated. This is exactly what the connectivists believe about the potential of the Web 2.0 social network. That through an extensive network of connections/ties knowledge is distributed, remixed and added back to the network in a cyclical fashion as people from diverse back grounds, cultures, disciplines and experiences recombine it with their existing knowledge base and return it to the network. New knowledge creation is said to be created through this process and empowered by social interaction and coactivity. The main thesis being presented here is that social capital facilitates the development of intellectual capital by affecting the conditions necessary for exchange and combination to occur.

3 Model building

From the literature above it is proposed that social capital is the *potential* that exists across a social network. "In a similar fashion, Verhagen, (2006) when speaking of the connectivist view of the social web, sees this *potential* "as using knowledge that you do not have at the ready, whose existence and usefulness you are aware of and to which you also have access". The amount of social capital is dependent on the *number* of connections (connectivism) to deliver the potential and the *quality* or nature of those connections. Strong connections will deliver bonding social capital and weak connections tend to deliver bridging social capital which can then in turn through more frequent connection and value gained from those connections, become bonding social capital. Bonding social capital is a higher level of social capital and delivers greater value because of the trust element involved. Intellectual capital has elements of potential also in the knowledge capability aspect. It is more focused on knowledge sharing and exchange and the outcome is new knowledge. Intellectual capital may develop using the same pathways as social capital and to some extent the same dynamics. Knowledge is shared through the social connections. Thus, the better the social connections the greater the potential for knowledge sharing is. The connectivisits would add, the more extensive and diverse the network the greater the possibility for new knowledge creation sharing and ultimately intellectual capital.

Moran and Ghoshal (1996) propose a mechanism for the development of intellectual capital from social capital via information benefits. These benefits can be amplified via Web 2.0 technologies. Information benefits occur in three forms: access, timing, and referrals.

"Timing" of information flows refers to the ability of personal contacts to provide information sooner than it becomes available to people without such contacts. "Referrals" are those processes providing information on available opportunities to people or actors in the network, hence influencing the opportunity to combine and exchange knowledge frequently include reputational endorsement for the actors involved (such as happens in Web 2.0 technologies through rating systems)-thereby influencing both the anticipated value of combination and exchange and the motivation for such exchange (see Granovetter, 1973, and Putnam, 1993). Much of the evidence for the relationship between social capital and intellectual capital highlights the significance of the relational dimension of social capital.

Figure 4 below shows knowledge sharing as the pivotal element that increases and creates social capital (cause and effect ,see Resnick, 2001; Williams, 2006) It also plays a similar role in the creation of intellectual capital. It is also the process that links social capital with intellectual capital facilitating the creation of new knowledge through exchange and recombination, driven by the ties of social capital. The entire process has been enabled by the Web 2.0 technologies.

4   Conclusion and suggestions for further research

It is generally accepted that the capacity of an organization to innovate lies in its capacity to generate new knowledge (Nonaka and Takeuchi, 1995; Nonaka, Toyama and Byosière, 2003). For this to be possible, knowledge sharing is considered a necessary condition (Nonaka and Takeuchi, 1995; Nonaka, von Krogh and Voelpel, 2006). It is suggested that Web 2.0 tools facilitate the development of social capital through knowledge sharing which in turn increases the potential to create intellectual capital. Web 2.0 is an important piece in this equation because it reinforces the notion that 'my connections help me' as it provides the means by which more connections can be made as well as facilitating the development of the social capital which in turn stimulates more sharing. It is suggested that organizations consider how they might use Web 2.0 technologies to tap into the power of social capital driven knowledge sharing.

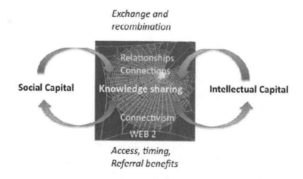

Figure 4: The relationship between social capital, knowledge sharing and intellectual capital in the 'Web 2.0' enabled environment.

As mentioned at the beginning of the paper, the constructs discussed have many components and this discussion has taken place at a high level, identifying some of the possible connections and relationship that exist in the conversion of social capital into intellectual capital via the Web 2.0 enabled information and knowledge sharing. Questions that remain include; which types of social capital are most important for the formation of intellectual capital, which types of social capital are best supported by Web 2.0 social networks, which types of Web 2.0 technologies best engender the building of social capital and knowledge sharing, and what types of knowledge is shared under what social circumstances?

References

Adler, P. and Kwon, S. (2002) "Social capital: Prospects for a new concept", Academy of Management Review, Vol 27, No.1, pp 17–40.

Bargh, J. and McKenna, K. (2004) "The Internet and social life", Annual Review of Psychology, Vol 55, No. 1, pp 573–590.

Bourdieu, P. and Coleman, J.S. (1991) Social Theory for a Changing Society, Westview Press, Boulder.

Bourdieu, P. and Wacquant, L. (1992) An Invitation to Reflexive Sociology, University of Chicago Press, Chicago.

Burke, M., Marlow, C., Lento, T. (2010) "Social Network Activity and Social Well-Being", CHI, April 10-15, Atlanta Georgia, USA

Casarez, V., Cripe, B., Sini, J. and Weckerle, P. (2009) Reshaping your business with Web 2.0, McGraw-Hill Companies, New York.

Coleman, J.S. (1988) "Social Capital in the Creation of Human Capital", American Journal of Sociology Supplement: Organizations and Institutions: Sociological and Economic Approaches to the Analysis of Social Structure, S95-S120.

Cross, R. and Cummings, J.N. (2004) "Tie and network correlates of individual performance in knowledge-intensive work", Academy of Management Journal, Vol 47, pp 928 - 937.

DiMicco, J. Millen, D.,Geyer,W., Dugan, C., Brownholtz, B., Muller, M. (2008) "Motivations for Social networking at Work", Proceedings of CSCW 08, November 8-12, San Diego, CA, USA.

Ellison, N., Steinfield, C. and Lampe, C. (2007) "The Benefits of Facebook "Friends:" Social Capital and College Students' Use of Online Social

Network Sites", Journal of Computer-Mediated Communication, Vol 12, pp 143–1168.

Fukuyama, F. (1995) Trust: Social Virtues and the Creation of Prosperity, Free Press, New York.

Granovetter, M.S (1973) "The strength of weak ties", American Journal of Sociology, Vol 78, pp 1360-1380.

Helliwell, J. F. and Putnam, R.D. (2004) "The social context of well-being", Philosophical Transactions of the Royal Society, Vol 359, pp 1435–1446.

Huysman, M. and Wulf, V. (2004) Social Capital and Information Technology, MIT Press.

Huysman, M. and Wulf, V. (2005) "Information technology in building and sustaining the relational base of communities", The Information Society, Vol 21, pp 81–89.

Jar-Der Luo. (2005) "Social network structure and performance of improvement teams", International Journal of Business Performance Management,Vol 7, No. 2, p 208

Kramer, R.M. and Tyler, T.M. (Eds.) (1996) 'Whither trust? Trust in organizations: Frontiers of theory and research', Sage, California.

Moran, P. and Ghoshal, S. (1996) "Theories of economic organization: The case for realism and balance", Academy of Management Review, Vol 21, pp 58-72.

Morris, R.M., Teevan, J., and Panovich, K (2010) "What Do People Ask Their Social Networks, and Why? A Survey Study of Status Message Q&A Behavior." CHI, April 10-15, Atlanta Georgia, USA

Nahapiet, J. and Ghoshal, S. (1998) "Social Capital, Intellectual Capital, and the Organizational Advantage", Academy of Management Review, Vol 23, p 242.

Nie, N. H. (2001) "Sociability, interpersonal relations, and the Internet: Reconciling conflicting findings", American Behavioral Scientist, Vol 45, No. 3, pp 420–35 .

Nonaka and Takeuchi (2006) "The knowledge creating company: How Japanese companies create the dynamics of innovation", Oxford University Press, London.

Nonaka, I., von Krogh, G. and Voelpel, S. (2006) "Organizational Knowledge Creation Theory: Evolutionary paths and future advances", Organization Studies, Vol. 27.

Nonaka, I., Toyama, R. and Byosiere, P. (2003) "A theory of organization knowledge creation: understanding the dynamic process of creating knowledge", Handbook of Organizational Learning and Knowledge, Oxford University Press, Oxford.

Putnam, R. (1993) "Making democracy work: civic tradition in modern Italy", Princeton University Press, Princeton.

Putnam, R. (2000) " Bowling Alone – The Collapse and Revival of American Community" New York: Simon & Schuster.

Resnick, P. (2001) "Beyond bowling together: Sociotechnical capital", HCI in the New Millennium, Addison-Wesley, Boston.

Schumpeter, J.A. (1934) "The Theory of Economic Development: An inquiry into profits, capital, credit, interest and the business cycle", Harvard University Press, Cambridge.

Schwier, D. and McCalla, G. (2003) "Social capital in virtual learning communities and distributed communities of practice", Canadian Journal of Learning and Technology, Vol 29, No. 3.

Steinfield, C., DiMicco, J., Ellison, N., Lampe, C. (2009) "Bowling Online: Socail Networking and Social Capital within the Organization", Proceedings of the fourth international conference on Communities and Technologies, June 25-27, University Park, PA, USA.

Vertovec, S. (2001) "Transnational social formations towards conceptual cross fertilization". Paper read at Transnational Migration: Comparative Perspectives, Princeton University.

Vivian, N and Fay, F. (2003) "Social Networks in Transnational and Virtual Communities", InSITE - "Where Parallels Intersect", Informing Science.

Wellman, B., Haase, A.Q., Witte, J. and Hampton, K. (2001) "Does the Internet increase, decrease, or supplement social capital? Social networks, participation, and community commitment", American Behavioral Scientist, Vol 45, No. 3, p 436.

Wikifailure: The Limitations of Technology for Knowledge Sharing

[1]Alexeis Garcia-Perez and [2]Robert Ayres
[1]Coventry University, UK
[2]Cranfield University, Shrivenham, United Kingdom
Originally published in the Proceedings of ECKM 2009

Editorial Commentary

In this case study, although the use of a Wiki for knowledge sharing was at first successful, use declined over time and attempts to stimulate re-use failed. Two key reasons were identified: a lack of critical mass of users and the time taken to access and use the Wiki. Given the 90:9:1 law of Social Media that states for any social tool; 90% of people will only read, 9% will read and occasionally contribute and only 1% will actively engage and participate; these findings are not too surprising. Two other rules of thumb emerge in this paper:*"Things never work as you expect"* and *"You can't force people to use Social Tools"*.

Abstract: Currently there is much interest in the use of Web 2.0 technologies to support knowledge sharing in organisations. Many successful projects have been reported. These reports emphasise how the use of such technology has unlocked new pathways for knowledge transfer. However, the limitations of Web 2.0 technologies are not yet well understood and potential difficulties may have been overlooked. This paper reports a case study of a Wiki which was implemented to support a group of researchers. Although belonging to the same institution, the group members were relatively dispersed and their research areas were disparate. Nevertheless a short study showed that there were benefits to be gained from sharing knowledge and that many of the researchers felt that a Wiki would be a good mechanism to support this. A Wiki was implemented and was initially very successful. A significant number of researchers contributed to the Wiki and almost all made use of it. However the usage declined over time and attempts to stimulate interest by providing incentives for contributions were unsuccessful. One year after launch use was minimal. A qualitative study was carried out to understand the reasons for this decline in use, and is reported in this paper. Responses suggest that two factors may have been particularly significant in explaining the failure of the system. One problem appears to have been a lack of critical mass. Only a small proportion of users are likely to contribute and there may be a threshold size for a community to be able to support a vibrant Wiki. Time also seems to have been an issue. Some respondents said that they simply were too busy to contribute to or use the system. Organisations which are considering the use of Web 2.0 technologies to support a knowledge management initiative should consider the likely impact of these factors in their own situation. Although technologies such as Wiki have great potential there are also pitfalls in undertaking such projects which are not yet well understood.

Keywords: Web 2.0, Enterprise 2.0, Wiki, knowledge sharing, knowledge management, collaborative technologies

1   Introduction

Sharing knowledge is one of the key processes that allow organisations to create value. In choosing their approach to the implementation of knowledge sharing strategies many organisations have been heavily influenced by the growing popularity of Enterprise Social Software – also known as Enterprise 2.0 (McAfee 2006). Jeed (2008) argues that using Web 2.0 tools or social software inside organisations improves collaboration, knowledge sharing and innovation.

Additionally, a review of the literature shows that it contains many more reports of successful Enterprise 2.0 initiatives than of failed ones. To mention just one of these technologies, successful knowledge management initiatives based on Wikis have been reported in a wide range of fields including software development, project management, technical support, sales and marketing, and research and development (Kussmaul and Jack 2008: 152). Thus, organisations are at risk of assuming that implementing one or more of those tools will be a silver bullet to overcome the limitations of their intra-organisational knowledge sharing processes.

This paper reports a case study where a Wiki was implemented as a knowledge sharing tool among a group of researchers working for a single organisation. The study is based on the findings of previous research, which indicated that members of the organisation had a wide range of areas of expertise and the willingness to share it. As face to face interaction was not possible on a regular basis, most of the researchers suggested they would share their knowledge using a technology such as a Wiki if it were available.

However, although the Wiki was initially successful it became clear, several months after its implementation, that it was not attracting the continued level of use that was originally hoped for. Apart from the occasional episode where use peaked dramatically due to extraneous factors (such as a competition or social event being advertised on the Wiki) the overall trend was towards a very low level of use. The research documented in this paper explores the reasons for the failure of this implementation.

The research concludes that more work needs to be done to understand the strengths and weaknesses of Enterprise 2.0 technologies such as Wikis so that they can be used appropriately.

The paper is structured as follows: section 2 provides an overview of the existing Enterprise 2.0 technologies in use as mechanisms for encouraging knowledge sharing between organisational participants. The rationale behind the selection of Mediawiki as the technology used to improve knowledge sharing within the organisation in this case study is detailed in section 3. Section 4 outlines the features included in the Wiki that was implemented. Section 5 reports the analysis of the usage statistics for the Wiki. The main reasons behind the lack of success of the Wiki as a knowledge transfer strategy in this case are explored in section 6, highlighting that these may also apply to other organisations.

2 Enterprise social software and intra-organisational knowledge transfer

AIIM (2009) defines Enterprise 2.0 as "a system of web-based technologies that provide rapid and agile collaboration, information sharing, emergence and integration capabilities in the extended enterprise". Organisations aiming at the implementation of strategies to elicit knowledge from experts and transfer it to practitioners using Enterprise 2.0 tools have a wide range of technologies at their disposal.

Enterprise 2.0 technologies can be grouped into two categories – those that support collaboration and those that allow the posting of information in a common space for other people to access it.

According to AIIM (2009) and Forrester Research (Yehuda et al. 2008), Enterprise 2.0 tools that support collaboration include:

- Wikis. Software that allows users to freely create and edit Web content using a Web browser. Given their relevance in the context of this research, Wikis will be referred to in more detail later in this and other sections.
- Social Bookmarking: A form of tagging done by individuals to communicate context and categorisation of information and knowledge resources that may not have been seen through a more formalized taxonomy-driven viewpoint.
- These principles have been implemented in a large number of knowledge sharing environments with a significant degree of success, according to Mika (2005).
- Collaborative Filtering: A method of determining the relevance of information and knowledge resources according to the actions of individuals.
- These systems often record the browse and search behaviours of users in order to assess the "value" of resources (Hahn and Subramani 2000).
- Social Networking: Dynamic "relationship" building, person-to-person connections – not necessarily "community" or collaboration.
- Facebook and LinkedIn are prime examples of consumer-facing Social Networking sites, now being implemented at intra-organisational level in many organisations.

2.1 Wikis: Success and failures

Enterprise 2.0 tools supporting a common information space include Blogs, RSS, and Wikis. Although the first two of these have also been considered successful Enterprise 2.0 technologies, they are less relevant to knowledge elicitation and transfer. However, this is not the case for Wikis. Wikis are particularly relevant as they allow contributors not only to post information into a public space but also collaborate in building a knowledge base by editing content that have been posted by others in the Wiki platform. As a result, Wikis have been exploited by many organisations for knowledge sharing.

Particularly successful has been the case of Sun Microsystems. Brown (2008) argues that – along with an extensive program for the training of staff in the use of the tool, Wikis have been developed and used as project management tools and community builders at Sun Microsystems, resulting in a significant step towards the implementation of further Enterprise 2.0 in that organisation.

Other successful initiatives have been recently reported. Wikis have been developed to support knowledge sharing in a wide range of projects not only within the scope of knowledge management (Selhorst, 2008) but also in related areas such as teaching and training (Raman et al., 2005) and the development of social networking strategies (Hustad and Teigland, 2008).. These have been encouraged by the result of studies such as that of Majchrzak et al. (2006) which, taking into account issues such as length of existence, number of users and frequency of accesses, concluded that corporate Wikis are sustainable. However, the literature shows almost no sign of negative experiences concerning the implementation of Wikis in organisations.

Nevertheless there is increasing concern regarding the importance of formulating a coherent foundational theory for the use of Wikis in organisations (Majchrzak, 2009).

3   The need for a Wiki as a knowledge sharing technology in a research environment

This case study was carried out in a research-oriented organisation among a group of researchers who were mainly working in areas such as engineering, applied science and management. The investigators undertook a study to see how these researchers exchanged knowledge and expertise and whether it could be improved.

There are in the organisation approximately 35 full-time researchers, whilst another 150 are part of the organisation on a part-time basis or for a fixed period of time, usually one year. The organisation is structured in departments that, although geographically dispersed, conduct research on related areas. As concluded by Garcia-Perez and Mitra (2008), interviews with staff revealed a wide spectrum of knowledge available in the community. However, work was possibly being duplicated and researchers were not supporting each other as they believed they would if they were more aware of each others' work. There was awareness of this problem at all levels within the organisation. However, because there was very little interaction among researchers on a regular basis, knowledge sharing was not taking place effectively.

There was a tacit agreement among all researchers about the need for more knowledge sharing, and most of them recommended the use of information and communication technologies as an appropriate way to address the problem given the organisational context. In particular, they mentioned the need for a Wiki and agreed to share their full profiles and relevant knowledge if such a technology was put in place.

The research reported here complements work conducted in 2007 with the aim of facilitating knowledge elicitation and transfer within the organisation using a Wiki. Some members of the community – including one of the authors of this paper, carried out the design and implementation of a Wiki as a collaborative, knowledge sharing tool within the organisation. The following sections describe the implementation of the Wiki and its adoption by the research community.

4   Design and Implementation of the Wiki

With the aim of enabling the community of researchers to share their knowledge two researchers (including one of the authors of this paper) agreed to design and implement a Wiki. In doing this they were following the recommendations of the interviewees, who had recently suggested that they would use the Wiki to share and reuse knowledge. The organisation's IT department agreed to provide the necessary server space, accounts and so forth that would be needed to support the Wiki. The community, lead by a development team, would only need to develop and maintain the Wiki.

4.1 Selection of features

Initial discussions led to a basic design of the structure of the Wiki, the features that it would include and the information and knowledge to be offered. These facilities were decided on as a result of the following:

- Needs expressed by members of the community during interviews, which led to the selection and implementation of the following facilities:
- People's profiles including a space for each researcher to publish their main areas of expertise, previous work experience and contact details. Most researchers had said they would be willing to share this information
- Group profiles, describing existing groups and communities of interest and practice within the organisation and their areas of research
- A 'How to...' section that everyone would contribute to with solutions to all sorts of known problems
- A bibliography space, where relevant documentation and web links would be shared
- Standard features of other Wikis implemented by known organisations or available on the Internet. These included:
- An area for researchers to do collaborative work, mostly developing documentation about the organisation and their research
- A joint calendar where all activities of common interest would be included
- A categorisation of pages and tagging features to facilitate search and retrieval of relevant information within the Wiki
- The investigators' views of what could potentially encourage researchers to exchange information and knowledge resources. Among these were:
- A message board to support the emergence of communities of interest within the organisation
- Chat facilities to make the interaction between researchers even easier
- A space used to discuss and organise social activities

Two of the researchers worked on the development of the first version of the Wiki from the beginning of 2007. This work involved the installation of Mediawiki, design of the interface and implementation of the above features. From April 2007, a larger team dedicated a significant amount of time to create as many pages as possible. By July 2007 the Wiki had begun to be known to the community. It had more than 100 pages with information covering all areas that had been mentioned by the community of researchers. Also, most of the features described above had been fully implemented, and these were supported by an interface that was designed to be attractive.

The Wiki was formally launched to the community in August 2007 with an email to all full-time researchers as the initial target of the initiative. The email not only included a description of the Wiki but also an invitation to a launch meeting a week later. More than 30 researchers attended the meeting, including some that had recently joined the organisation. Judging from the discussion that took place, the Wiki was embraced by the community as the tool needed by the organisation. Also it was confirmed that the community was still willing to use the technology as their main knowledge sharing mechanism. However, its usage over the following 18 months was not as predicted. The following section describes what followed the launch of the Wiki.

5   Use of the Wiki

In order to study and report the use of the Wiki a log file of accesses made was obtained from the IT department covering the period between 18 July 2007 (weeks before it was launched) and 14 January 2009. A number of different reports from several viewpoints were created and analysed using *Deep Log Analyzer*, a technology developed by Deep Software Inc., member of the Web Analytics Association. In a search for a better view of the diagrams generated by *Deep Log Analyzer*, some of these were exported to Microsoft Excel. The diagram in Figure 1 shows the fluctuations in the number of visits to the Wiki over the whole period:

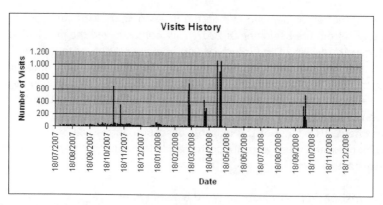

Figure 1: Visits per day during the whole period

In order to have a clearer view of the number of visits, an additional graph has been created by truncating the number of visits that exceeded the number of 50 per day. The resulting graph is shown in figure 2.

The total number of visits to the Wiki was over 15,000 in the period of 547 days being analysed. There were 200 visitors, considering as a visitor an IP address where a visit originates. Therefore, up to 200 people accessed the Wiki within the organisation or externally through a connection to its Virtual Private Network. These figures exceeded the initial expectations of the developers.

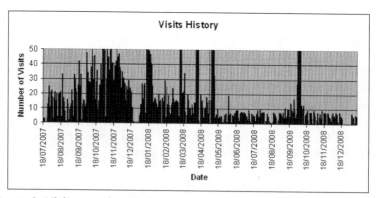

Figure 2: Visits per day during the whole period – truncated at the level of 50 visits

During its first month on the organisational domain (8 August to 8 September 2007) the Wiki had 362 visits coming from 46 visitors, as shown in the following diagrams:

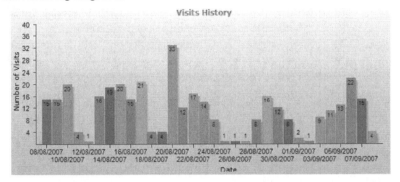

Figure 3: Number of visits to the Wiki per day during the first month after launch

The number of visits to the Wiki steadily grew between its launch in August 2007 and the beginning of 2008, with the expected low in its usage during the Christmas period in 2007.

However, in spite of its success during early stages, the analysis of visits and visitors over the whole period revealed several significant features, in particular:

- More than two thirds of the total number of visits originated from the same computer, which suggests that the visitor was either an administrator or a single user
- More than 13,000 of the total number of visits lasted less than 2 minutes.

Although these two issues were not noticeable during its first month (see Figures 3 and 4), they became areas of growing concern for the development team as time progressed. Additionally, only 14 of its users added some information to be shared with colleagues through their profiles.

In February 2008 the use of the Wiki began to decline. It became a pattern that most visits came from the same visitor. The Wiki never received more than 50 visits per week, except for six specific dates that can be seen from Figure 1 and can be explained as follows:

- Five of the peaks relate to the promotion and organisation of social activities which were advertised only in the Wiki
- The sixth and highest peak took place in May 2008 and is associated with an attempt to stimulate use of the Wiki by running a competition as a recovery strategy.

5.1   Looking for the reasons for the decline in use

A survey was conducted in February 2008 to explore the reasons for the low usage of the Wiki. With that aim, a questionnaire was designed, including three main questions. These were:

- Are you aware of the Wiki and the resources it contains?
- Have you ever used the Wiki?
- If so, was it a positive experience?
- Are you using the Wiki at present?
- Why?
- How could the Wiki be improved?

The questionnaire could be applied either face to face or using electronic means. The use of the Intranet or the Wiki itself would have introduced bias in the results - answers would be likely to come from those researchers who visited the Wiki on a regular basis. Therefore, one of the authors carried out interviews with members of the research community. A semi-structured interview would provide a richer insight following the topics outlined in the questionnaire above.

Eight researchers randomly selected from the community were interviewed. The key findings are outlined below.

Awareness of the Wiki:

- All interviewees were aware of the fact that a Wiki had been developed and deployed
- However, three of them accepted that they were not aware of the information the Wiki contained
- Three of the interviewees had contributed to the Wiki with at least one article

Use of the Wiki

- All but one interviewee had visited the Wiki at least once
- All of them described the Wiki as a very useful resource – including one person who had never visited the Wiki, but who mentioned that she had heard about it
- None of them had visited the Wiki in the month before the interview took place

Although no suggestions for improvements were made, issues relating to the lack of use included, in order:

- Time: Lack of time, being very busy with own work. Spending time in reading / contributing to the Wiki was seen as a lack of focus in their own work
- Information: Feeling that the Wiki did not have much to offer to those that had been in the organisation for more than 2 years. They had "survived without it", they argued. The information on the Wiki did not motivate them either to come back after a visit or to contribute new information
- Accessibility: Not having an easy, direct link to the Wiki on their computer desktop or the home page of the intranet hindered its usage

5.2   A recovery strategy: Rewarding contributions

Some of the issues which were uncovered by the survey, such as respondents' concern about time, could not be directly addressed by the development team. However, having funds available to improve the Wiki, a competition was designed to encourage new contributions in the hope that these would attract further users. Ideally, such contributions would also add value to the information already in the Wiki, and usage would increase. An iPod was offered by the organisation to the person who made the largest number of contributions over a three month period ending the 9 May 2008.

The motivation behind this competition was twofold:

- To encourage people to visit the Wiki in the hope that increased familiarity with the Wiki would in turn lead to greater use.

- To stimulate the production of new Wiki entries in the hope that this would help to produce a critical mass of relevant material and information to establish the Wiki as a useful resource for the researchers.

This strategy had a significant effect in the number of visits to the Wiki, taking it to its highest level (1,072 visits in one day), particularly towards the end of the period of the competition. However, immediately after the end of the competition the use of the Wiki fell sharply to the same levels that it was before, i.e. 40 visits per month mostly from one visitor, as seen in the diagram below:

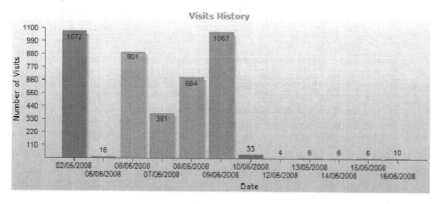

Figure 5: Number of visits per day before and after the end of the iPod competition (9 May 2008)

Although statistics do not allow an evaluation of the quality of contributions made during the period when the iPod competition was run, a review of the Wiki did not show a significant difference in the nature of resources. Visits to the wiki did not always result in new pages added, and the new contents were heavily concentrated in the section related to social activities and dominated by photographs.

The iPod competition failed to provide the expected results as a recovery strategy. The statistics during the following months (May 2008 until January 2009) show that the number of visits fell significantly over time. The following diagrams show the statistics for the last month being analysed.

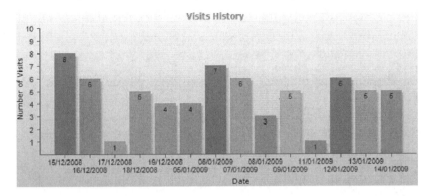

Figure 6: Number of visits per day during the last month of the analysis

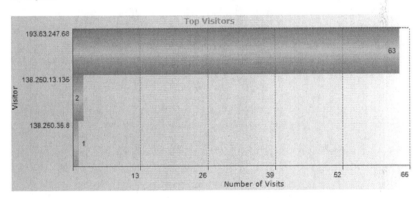

Figure 7: Number of visitors during the last month analysed. Note that 63 out of the 66 visits come from the same computer

The statistics in Figures 6 and 7 show that by the end of the period being analysed the use of the Wiki declined to sporadic visits from a small number of visitors. Again one particular visitor accounted for almost all the visits.

The initiative to stimulate use of the Wiki had thus not been successful. It is clear that in the short term the competition did result in a greatly increased number of visits and also encouraged a number of users to add a significant amount of further material. The fact that use declined sharply as

101

soon as the competition was over suggests that there were other problems rather than lack of awareness of what it offered or researchers not having posted information to the Wiki.

6 Discussion and conclusions

Obviously quantitative data on the number and duration of visits cannot be used directly to assess the value of the Wiki as a knowledge sharing mechanism. However consideration of the statistics does suggest that the Wiki was not achieving its purpose. An example of this is the fact that 91 visitors (46% of the total number of visitors) only visited the Wiki once, and 85% of the total number of visits only lasted less than 2 minutes. Although the number and duration of the visits does not necessarily reveal the nature of such visits, it is unlikely that someone who visited the Wiki once or navigated away within 2 minutes had taken part in successful knowledge exchange. Another example is the fact that more than two thirds of the total number of visits came from a single user (resulting in an average of 4 visits per day for the rest of the community), which indicates that the Wiki was not widely used.

This study confirmed the importance of a number of known issues in relation to the use of Wikis as knowledge sharing tools. These include:

- Time required to access/contribute to the body of information and knowledge embedded in the technology
- Critical mass: the balance visitors-contributors in some of the most successful Wikis, such as Wikipedia, is in a ratio of 1000 to 1 (Wikipedia 2009). Not all organisations can rely on such a low percentage of contributors to develop a technology that brings into the organisation tangible benefits in terms of knowledge sharing

However, the case study also found issues related to Enterprise 2.0 tools in general and Wikis in particular that, although relevant, had not been widely covered by the literature on the topic. These included:

- The validity of the technology as 'the right tool':
- In certain conditions an Enterprise 2.0 technology seems to be an appropriate solution to the sharing of knowledge within the organisation. This case study was representative of this situation: a rela-

tively small organisation formed by geographically distributed teams working on projects that were related in nature. Employees were very familiar with technologies and would be ready to adopt an organisation-wide strategy. All those who were involved with the design and implementation of the Wiki, as well as those users who had been interviewed prior to its implementation believed it would be successful. However, in practice the technology did not have the expected impact as a knowledge management strategy because employees did not use it as it was predicted.

- How the supposed 'willingness to share knowledge' is reflected in practice.

- The implementation of a Wiki should not be based solely upon employees' claimed willingness to share knowledge. Even if a study suggests that employees will share knowledge using a Wiki it does not necessarily mean that they will do so. Even at basic levels such as contact details or areas of expertise, there are several issues affecting the number and nature of contributions to the knowledge base. These may include barriers that potential users and developers of the technology did not consider before the design and implementation stages.

- The importance of carefully planned strategies to design, launch and keep the technology working, that consider issues such as communication and group dynamics.

- A Wiki can be seen as a framework to be used by communities of interest that may emerge and dissolve over time. Trying to force continuity of usage by a particular community that has changed its nature may have negative long term effects. Any recovery strategy should seek to encourage contribution and use of valuable resources.

Enterprise 2.0 technologies such as Wikis may provide the expected results in the elicitation and sharing of knowledge in certain conditions. However, they do not always work as expected. There are important challenges associated to the knowledge elicitation and transfer process.

The work reported in this paper suggests that there are reasons to be cautious in the implementation of Enterprise 2.0 tools. Even when the knowledge management team is working on fertile ground (e.g. users recommend the implementation of the technology and claim that it would be widely used), organisations cannot assume that implementing something like a Wiki is a solution to the problem of knowledge elicitation and sharing.

7   Acknowledgement

The authors would like to acknowledge the valuable help of those who worked on the design and implementation of the wiki, in particular Dr Chris Hargreaves and Dr Benoit Mangili.

References

AIIM – Association for Information and Image Management (2009), "What is Enterprise 2.0 (E2.0)?" [online], http://www.aiim.org/What-is-Enterprise-2.0-E2.0.aspx

Brown, S. (2008), "Wikis at Sun Microsystems: The Ongoing Evolution. *Find, Use, Manage and Share Information (FUMSI)*", [online], http://web.fumsi.com/go/article/share/3328

Davenport, T. H. and Prusak, L. (1998), *Working Knowledge*. Harvard Business School Press, Boston, Massachusetts

Deep Software. (2009), "Deep Log Analyzer: A Web Analytics Software", [online], http://www.deep-software.com/?ref=dla

Garcia-Perez, A. and Mitra, A. (2008), "Tacit Knowledge Elicitation and Measurement in Research Organisations: a Methodological Approach", *The Electronic Journal of Knowledge Management*. Volume 5 Issue 4, pp 373 – 386.

Hahn, J., and Subramani, M. R. (2000), "A Framework of Knowledge Management Systems: Issues and Challenges for Theory and Practice", *Proceedings of the 21st International Conference on Information Systems*. Brisbane, Australia. pp 302-312.

Hustad, E. and Teigland, R. (2008), "Implementing Social Networking Media and Web 2.0 in Multinationals: Implications for Knowledge Management", *Proceedings of the European Conference on Knowledge Management*. Southampton, UK. pp 323-331.

Jeed, M. (2008), "Can applying Web 2.0 to an organization make it faster, better? It's certainly making for more collaboration and knowledge sharing", *AIIM E-DOC Magazine*, January-February, [online], https://www.aiim.org/Infonomics/ArticleView.aspx?ID=34208

Kussmaul, C. and Jack, R. (2008), "Wikis for knowledge management: Business cases, best practices, promises and pitfalls". *In*: Lytras, M. D., Damiani, E. and Ordonez de Pablos, P. (Eds). *Web 2.0: The Business Model*, Springer, US. pp 147 – 165.

Majchrzak, A., Wagner, C. and Yates, D. (2006), "Corporate wiki users: results of a survey", *International Symposium on Wikis (WikiSym 06)*. Odense, Denmark.

Majchrzak, A. (2009). Comment: Where is the theory in Wikis? *MIS Quarterly*, Vol. 33. No. 1. pp 18-20.

McAfee, A. P. (2006) "Enterprise 2.0: The Dawn of Emergent Collaboration", *MIT Sloan Management Review*. Vol. 47. No. 3. pp 21–28.

Mika, P. (2005) "Ontologies are us: A unified model of social networks and semantics", *Proceedings of the 4th International Semantic Web Conference (ISWC 2005)*, Galway, Ireland, [online],
http://www.cs.vu.nl/~pmika/research/papers/ISWC-folksonomy.pdf

Raman, M., Ryan, T. and Olfman, L. (2005) "Designing Knowledge Management Systems for Teaching and Learning with Wiki Technology", *Journal of Information Systems Education*. Vol.16. No. 3. pp 311–320.

Selhorst, K. (2008) "Putting 'Knowledge Management 2.0' Into Practice – The process of setting up a Wiki as a Knowledge Management tool in a Public Library", *Proceedings of the European Conference on Knowledge Management*. Southampton, UK. pp 807-816.

Wikipedia. (2009) "About Wikipedia", [online],
http://en.wikipedia.org/wiki/Wikipedia:About

Yehuda, G., McNabb, K., Young, G.O., Burnes, S. and Reiss-Davis, Z. (2008) "Wikis and Social Networks are ready to deliver high value to your Enterprise", *Forrester TechRadar™ for I&KM Pros: Enterprise Web 2.0 for Collaboration*. Q4 2008.

Using Web2.0 Technology in Work Based Learning

Aboubakr Zade and Alan Durrant
Middlesex University, London, UK
Originally published in the Proceedings of ECEL 2009

Editorial Commentary

Work based learning has huge potential and Web 2.0 technology can effectively support such learning. This paper reports on the evaluation of the use of a Web 2.0 platform to support learning and teaching in a work based learning environment. One of the key recommendations, that I wholeheartedly agree with, is that you should allow people to use the tools, technologies and platforms that they are familiar with and that best suit their capabilities and needs. One size does not fit all.

Abstract: Although Web2.0 technologies are increasingly used in supporting learning and teaching in higher education, Work-based Learning is yet to achieve anticipated value from such technologies. Work Based Learning offers learning opportunities for professional practitioners; requiring special settings that link the learner, the university and the organization. Web2.0 is envisaged to provide suitable settings for Work Based Learning because it enables the creation of social environments, empowered by tools and technologies that facilitate learning, networking and collaboration among various stakeholders. This paper reports on the evaluation of a Web2.0 platform in supporting learning and teaching in a Work Based Learning environment. Middlesex University's School of Arts and Education launched a work based learning programme to allow professional practitioners to achieve an undergraduate qualification supported by a Web2.0- based platform for learning, networking and collaboration. The school launched the project reported in this paper to evaluate the impact of using the platform from three aspects: learning experiences, pedagogy and technology. In the first, we investigated how the platform impacted students' learning experiences and how learning experiences could be improved using Web2.0. In the second, we examined how successful the platform was in supporting the programme's learning outcomes, and how support for learning outcomes could be improved using Web2.0. In the third, we explored how successful the platform was in using Web2.0 technologies to support learning and teaching, and what other Web2.0 technologies could be used to improve the learning platform. The paper makes both practical and theoretical contributions. For practitioners it presents insights into designing and supporting Work Based Learning programmes and supporting teaching and learning using Web2.0 technologies. The unique capabilities and needs of individual professional practitioners studying through Work-based Learning programmes require a review of pedagogic strategy in light of the potential of Web2.0 technologies. The evaluation equally addresses a gap in the literature for empirical research into the use of Web2.0 technologies in supporting learning, networking and collaboration to facilitate Work Based Learning.

Keywords: Work based learning, e-learning, Web2.0, social technology, arts, education

1   Introduction

1.1   Our position on Work Based Learning

Work Based Learning (WBL) in the UK Higher Education system is at a watershed moment. The higher education policy drivers are forcing universities to give greater emphasis to their relationship to the economy (DfEE 1998 p7; DfES 2005) and characteristics of that relationship which include: partnerships agreement between University, student and employer; students are employees; needs of the work setting are central to the programme of study; prior learning is recognised and accredited; project work is focused on work context with employer support; university assesses negotiated programme against standard criteria (Boud 2001). This emphasis, we argue, has created an altered power dynamic where employers and other forms of work organizations have gained some measure of influence over the higher education curriculum. This altered relationship has caused an epistemological rearrangement for WBL:

> *Recent developments in work-based learning in higher education have prompted the question of epistemology. Unlike former versions of work based learning which were accommodated as practical expressions of subject-based epistemologies, the location of the current university-workplace relationship means there is no obvious epistemological home for it (Portwood 2007)*

If we broadly accept that the current norms in a subject-focus WBL gives prominence to the subject base, this infers the appropriateness of content-rich, consolidated, institutional e-learning and virtual learning environment (VLE) support. However, if we start to consider a more 'distributed' epistemological model where knowledge held in multiple sites, by individuals and organizations as both information and insights, we see that the monolithic, institutional VLE might be less helpful.

The development of professional practice programmes at Middlesex University is based on a constructivist model of learning, where, we believe, knowledge is accessed from diverse sources and connected into relationships by learners (Downes 2007). The university becomes less of a knowledge repository, and more a place to train brains to develop rich networks of sources and resources, and to become practiced at connecting these in new knowledge-schemas.

Based upon the WBL curriculum, we can see in Table 1 how the generic professional practice programmes are altering the epistemological basis, and learning and teaching interactions, between, what we slightly tongue-in-cheek refer to as WBL 1.0 and WBL 2.0.

Table 1: Generations of Work Based Learning (see Critten & Moteleb 2007)

FIRST GENERATION WBL (1.0)	SECOND GENERATION WBL (2.0)
Tutor led/supported WBL accredited Programmes with tutor/line manager taking lead	Tutor/line manager enables group of students/employees (learning communities) to recognize their own learning networks within which to create own development projects. Within this network tutor/line manager is also a fellow WBL learner who likewise makes available his/her learning network
Administration helps WBL learner surmount the hurdles in the learning process	
Technology support via the monolithic VLE primarily supporting individual learners	Administration works with all those within a learning network to chart their 'learning trajectory' which is the subject – individual or collectively- of accreditation
	Social technology which supports and includes individuals' own learning networks and integrates them in such a way as to make explicit how learning can be connected up and accredited within an Institutional context

We can now identify a newly emerging model of WBL where the hegemony of the subject discipline is reformed by the learner, through access and development of their professional networks, connected into new knowledge-schemas. This new perspective gives prominence to the learner constructing their own professional persona, and using a rich and individualised set of sources and resources.

It is hard to say whether Web 2.0 technologies caused this change, but it is clear that there is an elegant connection between this epistemological idea, and the emergence of Web 2.0. We took this connection as an opportunity to pilot the use of Web 2.0 to test out how we might foster greater connectivity between learners and their networks.

This paper presents the evaluation of a Web2.0 platform using Emerald *InTouch* – in supporting learning and teaching for Middlesex Centre for Excellence in Work Based Learning (CEWBL). Accordingly, this paper proceeds with providing the project context and goals in Section 2. Then in section 3, it presents the evaluation of the project from three aspects: (1) learning experiences, (2) pedagogy and (3) technology. Finally, the paper concludes and discusses future development in Section 4.

1.2   Project context and goals

Needs of the economy has become one of the most significant UK higher education policy areas over the last 5 years. The turn of the millennium saw an unexpectedly high number of centres of excellence relating to work and the workplace, and this foreshadowed the multi-million pound Strategic development funding (SDF) bids to re-orientate higher education onto the needs of work and the employer (HEFCE 2007). Most recently, in 2008, the Higher Education Funding Council for England (HEFCE) capped the student numbers for traditional courses while offering new funding for employer co-funded student numbers.

These, and other initiatives have strengthened WBL across the higher education sector, and set a major challenge to Universities to move to a more structured relationship with employers and the workplace. For example, by providing Foundation Degrees and extensions to full honours degrees by work based learning routes.

1.1.1 Changing WBL pedagogy and Web 1.0 / Web 2.0

For WBL in higher education the challenge has been to reconsider its traditional roots and to respond to this challenge. WBL grew out of curriculum principles located in Continuing Education, and its pedagogies that gave prominence to adult learners (Knowles 2005). The underlying pedagogy of WBL gave prominence to certain principles, dominant amongst these are the accreditation of prior learning, both certificated (APL) and experiential (APEL). These continue to be appropriate for experienced, 'established' professionals and practitioners but have less utility for newly emerging, 'establishing' workers graduating from Foundation Degrees and progressing onto WBL undergraduate degrees. With greater likelihood of students having little or no work experience on which to base APL/APEL, it has been necessary for curriculum developers to adapt WBL pedagogy to learning and teaching tasks that gives greater emphasis to learning in action and less to learning on action (Schön 1983, 1987).

With WBL students dispersed in various workplaces, the principles of Web 1.0 that underpin the monolithic institutional VLE have always been stretched to accommodate the students' needs. The focus of WBL is on reflection and actions rather than subjects and content, which place strains on VLE technologies. To this we must add the greater emphasis placed on the development of organisation communities of learners (Lave & Wenger 1991) where WBL students are communicating and sharing with co-workers on the periphery of their course rather than with other students. This focus on 'work' communities of practice in the WBL curriculum remains completely unsupported by the monolithic VLE, posited on the notion that shared learning experiences only take place between enrolled students.

The ideas of wider, work-based community of learning, and the process of reflection in action, unsupported by Web 1.0 and the institutional VLE, are elegantly provided for by Web 2.0 with its focus on communities, connections (Downes 2007), personalisation and a distributed set of tolls, chosen for appropriateness by the individual student or group rather than the tutor.

The decision to pilot the use of Web 2.0 to support WBL students was driven by the principles and issues identified above. Other institutions are currently exploring the potential of Web 2.0, many funded via JISC (JISC 2009).

1.2.1   The project

This paper presents the evaluation of a Web 2.0-based platform in supporting learning and teaching for Middlesex Centre for Excellence in Work Based Learning (CEWBL). As a leading centre in developing and rewarding teaching and learning for professional practitioners, the Centre seeks to be at the leading edge in using Information and Communication Technologies to support learning and teaching, for WBL students and staff especially when working away from base. Emerald InTouch offers learners and teachers an online platform and a Web-based social space designed to support learning, networking and collaboration based on Web2.0 technologies and tools. A pilot project was therefore set to support professional practitioners studying for BA (Hons) Professional Practice (BAPP) with the School of Arts and Education during the academic year 2007-2008. This paper presents an evaluation of this pilot project.

InTouch is evaluated in the context of its use as part of the BA (Hons) Professional Practice (BAPP). BAPP is delivered by the Institute of Work Based Learning (WBL) at Middlesex University. The programme offers a WBL route for professional practitioners – in creative and cultural industries – who wish to progress from professional diplomas, certificates and foundation degrees to a BA (Hons) level. BAPP Students can therefore pursue the final year of BAPP by linking their learning to their professional development. The programme is based on 'professional practice' whereby practitioners recognise their professional skills and networks, reflect on their practice and seek to advance and enhance professional knowledge and skills within and beyond their current practice. The BAPP programme team at Middlesex University seeks to guide professional practitioners on BAPP by helping them recognise and reflect on their practice, and accredit them accordingly.

It is within this context that InTouch was introduced to support learning and collaboration among professional practitioners studying for BAPP and the programme team. Although students had the opportunity to take part in few taught sessions throughout the programme, BAPP is mainly based on self-directed learning, to allow busy practitioners, who cannot always come to university, to pursue further qualifications. InTouch was used to support learning, networking and collaboration among BAPP students through a range of Web2.0 technologies and tools, such as Blogs, Wikis, RSS. Accordingly, students were invited to use InTouch to build communities of practice (Wenger 1998; Wenger et Al. 2002). By communities of practice we mean groups of students built around areas of interest, engage in conversations, create knowledge repositories, collaborate on projects and network with other professionals around topics of interests as well as academic research and WBL topics.

The aim of this evaluation was to investigate how successful was this Web 2.0-based platform in supporting learning and teaching among professional practitioners studying for BAPP and the programme team during the academic year 2007-2008, and to explore potential improvements for future cohorts. The evaluation covered three aspects:

- Learning experiences: How successful was using InTouch in supporting learning outcomes, and how can support for learning outcomes be improved using InTouch?
- Pedagogy: How did InTouch impact students' learning experiences and how can students' learning experiences be improved using InTouch?
- Technology: How successful was InTouch in using social technologies to support learning in students' views, and what other social technologies could be used to improve the learning platform?

For the evaluation of the first of these aspects, we interviewed a third of the professional practitioners, after a year studying on the programme, in the context of the programme objectives. In the second aspect, we used interviews with the Programme Director and industry consultants and documentation review of learning outcomes of the programme. In the third aspect, we assessed *InTouch* and its potential in supporting learning outcomes of the programme . Details of this evaluation is presented in Section 3.

Recommendations based on the evaluation of using *InTouch* in supporting learning and teaching in BAPP from the perspective of these three aspects are presented in the conclusion and future development in Section 4.

2 Evaluating the use of Web2.0 platform for WBL

2.1 Learning experiences

Interviews confirmed, what was evident in our observations of students' participations on *InTouch*. Students did not use the full potential of the platform in improving their learning experiences. Interviewees stressed that they regularly used other Web2.0 platforms to network on personal levels, and thus could see a potential for using it for professional purposes. However, they strictly throught of *InTouch* as an e-learning platform and thus missed the opportunity to use it in supporting and linking their learning with their professional development and practice. Moreover, they did not relate to peers on *InTouch* because of lack of connections and lack understanding into how they can benefit from networking and learning collaboratively with their peers. This was particularly evident in the scarce and generally 'superficial' participation in different communities on the platform.

The nature of WBL activities during the first two terms partially contributed to this as learning activities were primarily related to issues that were unique to students (e.g. their profiles, 'Learning Agreements' and 'Professional development themes'). As a result, they did not show interest in sharing experiences on the platform. Yet it made more sense to them to share it with their personal networks through other Web2.0 platforms or offline.

To improve students' learning experiences using *InTouch* and other Web2.0 platforms and technologies, it is therefore important for students to be able to link learning outcomes and activities in WBL to their professional development and networks. For example, they should be encouraged to bring their own professional networks into conversations around ideas about their own understanding of the terms 'practice' and 'professionalism' within their own practice.

More importantly, learning experiences could be improved using InTouch and other Web2.0 platforms if students linked their learning with their practice. Students should be encouraged to link to their external networks (e.g. 'networks for artists) and to their daily life and work. They could also link *InTouch* and other Web2.0 platforms to their work. For example, one student who is engaged in a children theatre company envisaged using Web 2.0 to link to children and their parents through her blog to share ideas.

InTouch and other Web2.0 platforms add a 'social' aspect in supporting learning off-campus as they include social tools that students are familiar with in their day-to-day personal networking. For example, students can use tweeter to their professional blogs about ideas or experiences they have 'as it happens'. Students should also be encouraged to link their presence on *InTouch* and other Web2.0 platforms to their communities of practice, which makes more sense to them and brings more value to them.

2.2   Pedagogy

Interviews with programme director and industry consultants further confirmed and clarified findings from students' interviews and review of BAPP learning outcomes. WBL learners usually create their own programme of study based on their work experiences (which is very difficult to do for a young person with little experience), they require a certain independence of mind. As a result, students were not able to grasp anticipated value from *InTouch* and Web2.0 platforms, especially in supporting them to achieve the learning outcomes of BAPP. Students' participations were insufficient to stimulate and sustain valuable conversations and collaboration towards achieving the learning outcomes of the programme. Much of students' participations in various online communities on *InTouch* were 'superficial', and hence did not help in achieving the anticipated learning outcomes.

The nature of WBL activities required from students partially contributed to this because it required them to reflect primarily on issues that they could not relate to their peers. Students were envisaged to have better ability to achieve learning outcomes and have a much better learning experience, if they were to be given more help to make sense of their experiences within their own settings rather than within an "artificial setting". Therefore, students should be supported and encouraged in building, reflecting and refining their own portfolios in relation to their communities and networks. Similarly, tutors should be building, reflecting and refining their portfolios in relation to their students, as peers on the network. This is a prime challenge for WBL programmes' designers.

Moreover, learning and networking platform need to cater for the different identities of participants. Students on BAPP were grouped into two main categories: (1) more experienced practitioners and (2) novice (less experienced) practitioners. Each group had different capabilities and hence different needs. The first group have been practicing for a considerable amount of time, exposed to more professionals and worked in their communities and industries, and thus had a better grasp of their professions and its requirements. They had better understanding, and were more likely able to better recognise and express: where they were in comparison to their peers and where they wanted to be. These more experienced practitioners also relatively established their professional networks. Accordingly, they were pursuing BAPP to get their work recognised and accredited and to obtain higher qualifications to advance their careers within their specific domains. The less experienced practitioners, however, were students who were yet to achieve level 3 work. Although students who belonged to this group were also seeking professional development to advance their careers, they had yet to fully grasp their professions and its requirements. They were less confident when it came to expressing where they were and where they wanted to be in terms of their careers. Students who belonged to this group were yet to establish their professional networks.

Building on these findings, we came to the conclusion that supporting and motivating different 'types' of students in BAPP in particular (and WBL in general), requires a fundamentally different approach to learning and teaching, and consequently to designing and developing IT systems that support it. A new model for BAPP learning, teaching and assessment emerged from these conversations. This model was envisaged to allow and encourage students to represent their work environments and their networks and relationships the way they see it; as depicted in Figure 1.

As shown in figure 1, the programme would actually join the professional practitioners and their networks rather than expect them to join the programme and its students. Accordingly, students should be allowed and encouraged to develop their learning portfolios by building on this basis; linking it to their previous experiences, current work projects and their vision to where they will be in the future, rather than building learning portfolios that merely take superficial 'slices' of their work; in isolation of their actual work and communities. Similarly support for achieving learning outcomes could be improved by allowing the assessment strategy to evolve with change in the WBL environment and students' needs. Instead of assessing only (vertical) 'slices' of students' learning experiences, the programme assessment should evolve in a way that could evaluate students' lifelong learning across the past, present and future (horizontal).

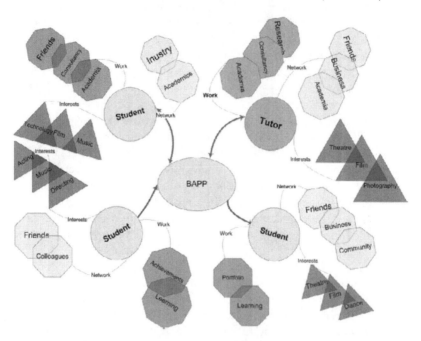

Figure 1: BAPP new learning and teaching model

To this end each student can build his/her portfolio online, showing context for their work and linking it to work in their field. Assessment of students' portfolios could also be online. Once they complete their programme, students should be able to continue building and refining their portfolios to help their careers and lifelong learning. In this way the programme would not only cater for different 'types' of students, but will enable each student to keep his/her own identity allowing them for a personalised programme that caters for individual capabilities and needs, especially as they are working remotely.

2.3   Technology

Drawing on results from the evaluation of the first two aspects and based on students' interviews a first version[1] of *InTouch* was assessed. Furthermore, based on envisioned improvements in the first two aspects and the interview with the programme director a new Beta version of *InTouch* was assessed. The first version of *InTouch* used Web2.0 technologies to support learning, collaboration and networking among students. It offered Blog technology for instance to enable each participant (i.e. student, programme adviser, etc.) to create their own Blog, where they publish background information about themselves and articles about their ideas and views on certain topics. It also allowed for communities interest groups to be set as blogs around relevant discussion topics, where interested individuals could join and participate. Participants could also upload useful documents on the platform. It offered Wiki technology to enable participants to collaboratively work on projects or to create online portfolios. Moreover, it used RSS technology to enable participants to subscribe to feeds of interest, and tagging technology for each publisher to attribute some keywords to their articles. The platform also allowed participants to flag a page if they thought it contains content that is obscene or inappropriate.

Although students were aware of Web2.0 technologies and some were using it to different levels, they faced technological challenges which affected the use of *InTouch* to support them in enhancing their learning experiences and achieving learning outcomes. These challenges were attributed to the user interface and navigation difficulties, and to lack of understanding of the platform and how it can support professional development and learning. Students found it difficult to use the first version of *InTouch* because Navigation was perceived difficult and the interface was not user-friendly. For example, some of the participants didn't know how to reach certain spaces and/or functionalities easily. This problem was magnified by limited technical skills of many of the students. In the first version of *InTouch* it was also difficult for the average user to do some functions such as linking to an external website or Blog. These problems made it difficult

---

[1] This evaluation was based on an earlier version of *InTouch* that was used by this student cohort. However, a newer version *InTouch* 2.0 Beta was released while writing this evaluation.

for students to participate in conversations and grasp anticipated value from the platform. Furthermore, some students were not aware of security levels provided by the platform and thus raised privacy issues as they did not have enough trust to publish their work on the platform. Part of this was because students could not know who is on *InTouch* at any moment in time. However, the same students felt more comfortable with other Web2.0 technologies such as Facebook.

Evaluation of *InTouch* also confirmed findings from the interviews; there were lack of awareness and understanding among participants into how can the platform be used to support their learning experiences. For example, it was not clear for many students how to use the different areas offered on the first version of *InTouch* (e.g. Your Activity, Your Blog, Your files, Your Pages, Your Resources, Your Profile). More importantly, students perceived *InTouch* to be only for university work and not for socialising with their peer students on BAPP. This has impacted the way participants perceive other professional practitioners on the platform. As a result, students separated between the use of *InTouch* and the use of other Web2.0 technologies such as Facebook.

The first version of *InTouch* could be improved on three levels. First, user interaction and ownership needs to be improved by giving user more control on their interfaces, more help on navigation and functions, and more information. Many Web2.0 based platforms now give users control to organise their interfaces the way that suits them (e.g. iGoogle). Therefore, it is a user expectation to be able to re-organise their interfaces on *InTouch* to facilitate their and their visitors' navigation through their pages. Second, the value of *InTouch* to students could be improved by providing them with other useful communication and collaboration technologies and tools. Besides Blogs, Wikis and RSS, there are plenty of Web2.0 technologies and tools that can enrich students' experiences on InTouch. For example, tagging technologies (see Del.icio.us) can help students share bookmarks to useful resources on the Internet. Creating a tagging cloud (see Del.icio.us) for each user, students can relate to others based on shared interests and skills. Also, sharing multimedia files (e.g. photos and videos) of relevant work can be useful to students. Third, the value of *InTouch* as a platform for learning, collaboration and networking could improve by allowing users to integrate it with other platforms, technologies and tools they were using in their personal and professional environments. For example, enhancing users' experiences by giving them more control to connect *InTouch* to other personal and/or professional networks, or allowing users to add and/or create external widgets and mashups on *InTouch*. In addition, interactions could be improved by providing users by useful information such as who else is logged on while they are on *InTouch*.

The new Beta version of *InTouch* provides an improved platform to support learning, networking and collaboration. However, how flexible the new platform will be in catering for different needs and capabilities of students and how it can be incorporated in their day-to-day activities is yet to be tested.

3   Conclusion and future development

This paper presented an evaluation of a Web 2.0-based platform in supporting learning and teaching among professional practitioners studying for BAPP and the programme team during the academic year 2007-2008, and explored potential improvements for future cohorts from three aspects: (1) learning experiences, (2) pedagogy and (3) technology.

For the evaluation of the first of these aspects, we interviewed a third of the professional practitioners, after a year studying on the programme, in the context of the programme objectives. The general consensus among interviewees was that *InTouch* as a social technology could be useful for their learning and careers. However they have not been able to grasp anticipated value from the technology for different reasons, prominent is their inability to link this Community of Practice (CoP) to their personal and professional environments.

In the second aspect, the main findings from interviewing the Programme Director and reviewing the learning outcomes of the programme were (a) the programme and hence supporting technology need to cater for different needs and capabilities of practitioners studying on the programme, and therefore (b) a review of learning and assessment strategy in the context of Work Based Learning (WBL) is required. These findings were reinforced through interviews with Industry Consultants.

In the third aspect, we assessed *InTouch* and its potential in supporting learning outcomes of the programme. Improvement to *InTouch* could be

achieved through enhancing user interaction, adding more tools and functions to the platform and enabling integration with external Web2.0 platforms and technologies. In addition, we explored potential use of *InTouch*
and other Web2.0 technologies for marketing through engaging with pros-
pect WBL students.

Although professional practitioners studying in BAPP had different levels of
experience with IT, they indicated that they were familiar and comfortable
to some extent in using other Web2.0 technologies and tools, and hence
they thought it could be useful for supporting their professional development and learning. In that respect, students' learning experiences can be
improved using Web2.0 technologies on the levels of (a) their learning, (b)
their careers and more importantly in (c) linking the two together.

WBL learners created their own body of knowledge through making sense
of their own experiences. In this, they needed to be able to create their
own platform, where they could connect to other platforms, technologies
and tools to help them plan and achieve their learning and professional
development goals. This happens primarily within their communities of
practice and networks, while their WBL community is only another space
where they can choose to meet other students who are pursuing the same
programme. Students should be able to make sense of these environments, and choose to link it together and connect to it in the way they see
best suits their capabilities and needs. Therefore, a WBL environment
should be ready to connect to these students' environments rather than
asking them to be part of it. *InTouch* 2.0 Beta is more lenient than the first
version in allowing users to link to other platforms and networks. However,
it can be further improved by allowing users to integrate different tools
together – what is known as mashups.

Improvement in developing WBL systems has to address the issues raised
in students' learning experiences, pedagogy and technology. For this a
fundamentally new approach for learning, teaching and assessment is required to address the different nature and needs of BAPP students. This
approach should also be able to evolve with changes in the WBL environment and students' needs. Therefore we can summarise our recommendations, particularly for practitioners in the following points:

- Review the current WBL strategy and work-out a new value-based strategy that can encompass new insights into needs and capabilities of learners, their networks and CEWBL. The foci of such a strategy is on establishing and developing professionals.
- Develop new pedagogic strategy in teaching, learning and assessment that is aligned with the WBL strategy and that capitalises on state-of-the-art information and communication technology in a way that brings value to learners. This is envisaged to be achieved by helping learners create/reflect on their professional persona and recognise/map to their professional networks.
- Develop an IT strategy to support the overall WBL strategy and the pedagogic strategy, in a way that allows learners to use tools, technologies and platforms that they are familiar and comfortable with and that enable the programme and its advisors to be part of the learners' network (as another – focal – node in the network)
- Develop a new corresponding curriculum that is aligned with the pedagogic strategy and uses state-of-the-art information and communication technology to help learners achieve learning outcomes by liking their learning to their practices. Potential curriculum streams include: (a) the Networked Professional; (b) Professional Thinking and Inquiry; and (c) the Reflective Professional .
- Create a presence of BAPP on Web2.0 platforms to be able to communicate with learners and their networks and to act as a focal point for these communities of practice and networks. This is also envisaged to create a social marketing environment for the programme and WBL in general.

We are creatures of habit. In piloting InTouch we sought to connect learners to each other and to sources and resources. However, we in fact created another centralised, monolithic structure, which did not properly capture the original intention of connecting learners.

The evaluation has prompted us to develop the curriculum further, giving greater prominence to the creation of connections by aligning learning, teaching and assessment to this aim. We have articulated three principles through which learning, teaching and assessment will be constructed, and these are:

1. Reflection in / on action / experience (deepening knowledge)

2. Practising / knowledge in action – (expanding knowledge)

3. Collaboration (extending Knowledge)

Through these principles we are working on activities that will strengthen and give greater focus upon, and opportunities to create connections between learners and their professional settings in two ways. Firstly, by interacting with students' existing use of Web 2.0. Secondly by providing suggested technologies implicated by specific learning tasks. These technologies are now less likely to be owned and managed by the University and more likely to be free on the web and/or controlled by the individual students. Clearly there are issues of concern for the University, however we will need to resist the desire to control, and embrace the opportunities presented by Web 2.0 in our new, technology-enabled, networked world.

References

Boud D. & Solomon N. (Eds.) (2001) Work-Based Learning: A New Higher Education? UK: SRHE

Critten P. & Moteleb A. (2007) 'Towards a Second Generation of Work Based Learning – Supporting Social Knowledge', Proceedings of the Work Based Learning Futures Conference

Knowles M. S., Holton E. F. III, & Swanson, R. A. (2005). The adult learner: The definitive classic in adult education and human resource development (6th ed.). Burlington, MA: Elsevier

Portwood, D. (2007) Towards an Epistemology of Work-Based Learning: Eliciting clues from work based projects in Young, D & Garnett, J. (Eds) Work-based Learning Futures Bolton: Universities Vocational Awards Council.

DfEE (1998) The Learning Age: A renaissance for a New Britain. Department for Education and Employment, Sheffield

DfES 14-19 Education and Skills White paper (2005) Department for Education and Employment [Source: http://www.dfes.gov.uk/publications/14-19educationandskills/ accessed: 15/6/2009]

Downes S. (2007) An Introduction to Connective Knowledge in Hug T. (ed.) (2007): Media, Knowledge & Education - Exploring new Spaces, Relations and Dynamics in Digital Media Ecologies. Proceedings of the International Conference held on June 25-26, 2007. November 27, 2007.

HEFCE (2007) Strategic Development Fund. Bristol: Higher Education Funding Council for England.

JISC funded projects focused on Web2.0 [Source: http://www.jisc.ac.uk/whatwedo/topics/web2.aspx accessed: 2/9/2009]

Schön D. (1983) The Reflective Practitioner: How professionals think in action. London: Temple Smith.

Schön D. (1987) Educating the Reflective Practitioner. San Francisco: Jossey-Bass.

Lave J. & Wenger E. (1991) Situated Learning: Legitimate peripheral participation Cambridge: CUP

Wenger E. (1998) Communities of Practice, UK: Cambridge University Press

Wenger E., McDermott R. & Snyder W. (2002) Cultivating Communities of Practice, US: Harvard Business School Press

Let Students Talk: Web 2.0? Web 3.0? Or None?

Nazime Tuncay[1] and Mustafa Tuncay[2]
[1]Near East University, Nicosia, North Cyprus
[2]Atatürk Teacher Training Academy, Nicosia, North Cyprus
Originally published in the Proceedings of ECEL 2009

Editorial Commentary

The purpose of the study discussed in this paper was to discover the Web 2.0 preferences of students and their expectations from Web 3.0 technologies. Some interesting points emerge. First, students tend to see the tools as social networking tools and not as learning tools. Second, the world is moving so fast, that when it comes to Social Tools and Web 2.0, students know more than their teachers and their parents. We can all learn from each other and it seems to me that there is a wonderful opportunity here for two way learning.

Abstract: Students in 21st century have changed radically with the evolving technology and Web 2.0 tools. They are no longer the students the current educational system was designed to teach. Using technologies that support high levels of accessibility web tools, and providing students with choices are of the highest importance. Although many students engage with Web 2.0 technologies on a daily basis, they view them as social networking tools and they have different expectations from Web 3.0 tools. A questionnaire was created to find Web 2.0 tools preferences of high school students and university students (which was posted on Surveymonkey.com). 210 high school students and 231 university students, in North Cyprus, have answered the questionnaire. 15 high school students and 15 university students were chosen randomly for one-to-one interviews with the researchers. Interviews were carried out to drive out students' expectations from Web 3.0 technologies. Students' responses in the questionnaires differed significantly based upon students' schools: High school students were mostly using web tools for communication with their friends and university students were using web tools mostly for communication with their family members. Some of the other interesting results of this research are: Facebook is the most commonly used Web 2.0 tool and Hi5 is the second most commonly used web tool. In the interviews, some of the interesting answers of the students were: "Web 2.0 tools should have better group meeting audio systems"; "They should contain Multilanguage support" and "they should have better group meeting audio system". Most of the students said that they want to learn how to use Web 2.0 tools, although their parents restrict themselves. In conclusion, lots of results were obtained by "letting the students talk". Researchers found that "blended education" programs would be the best way to improve high school students and university students Web 2.0 training needs. Teachers and parents should be informed about the benefits of the usage of web tools in education. These results should provide insight to educators and cause them to rethink and analyze their Web 2.0 choices for their courses. It presents a framework for Web 3.0 projects. Further studies of the researchers would be "Teachers web 2.0 choices and their expectations from Web 3.0 tools".

Keywords: Students, Web 2.0 tools, Web 3.0 tools, education

1   Introduction

1.1   Web tools

Just as everyone was getting used to the term Web 1.0 and Web 2.0; Web 3.0 is making its way to the front seat of many conferences. *"It is hard to define web tools"* (Elkind 2009; Nova, 2009, MacManus, 2007), what is Web 3.0? Which tools can be classified as Web 3.0? There are many different definitions about Web 3.0, and there seems to be a lot more challenging in the following years. Web 1.0 is the name of the tools like; Double-Click, Ofoto , Akamai, MP3.com, Britannica Online, personal websites, evite, domain name speculation, optimization,page views, screen scraping, publishing, content management systems and directories (taxonomy) (O'Reilly, 2005). Web 2.0 is the name of the tools like Google AdSense, Flicker , BitTorrent ,Wikipedia, blogging, upcoming.org and EVDB, search engine optimization, cost per click, web services, participation, wikis and tagging ("folksonomy"), stickiness (O'Reilly, 2005). In 2004, Web 2.0 became a collective term for a mass movement in society: *"A movement toward new forms of user engagement supported by Web-based tools, resources, services and environments"* (Alexander, 2006). *Web 2.0, sometimes referred to as the "read/write Web", provides online users with interactive services, in which they have control over their own data and information* (Madden and Fox, 2006 and Maloney, 2007). *Multimedia tools*

125

like podcasts and video casts are increasingly popular in medical schools and medical journals (Giustini, 2006). Although, lots of researchers still argue today, the advantages of Web 2.0 tools; new tools are necessary to keep up with the rapid changes in the technological world.

Web 3.0 is pursuing its way with the web tools like Twine and Semantic Web 3.0. It is going to be the name of many new Web tools. *"Web 1.0 was the content Web, Web 2.0 has generally been regarded as the social Web; and Web 3.0 is the location-aware and moment-relevant Internet"* (Todd, 2009).According to Cho (2008), *Web 3.0 is based on "intelligent" web applications using: Natural language processing, machine-based learning and reasoning, intelligent applications. "Web 3.0 will ultimately be seen as applications which are pieced together and can run on any device, PC or mobile phone. The applications are very fast and they're very customizable. Furthermore, the applications are distributed virally: literally by social net-works, by email"* (MacManus, 2007).

Use of web 2.0 technologies such as blogs and wikis in the classroom learning environment can be effective at increasing students' satisfaction with the course. It can improve their learning, their writing ability, and it can increase student interaction with other students in high schools and in universities. It changes the students' role from passive to active learners, allowing them to better create and retain knowledge (Maloney, 2007). With Web 2.0, the very nature of student work has changed from student-teacher interaction to student-community interaction (Johnson, 2009).

With the evolving technology and Web tools, schools, students and teach-ers have changed radically. Usage of social networking sides like Facebook, Youtube, Slideshare, Hi5 and Flicker and social bookmarks like del.icio.us and Furl have become widespread among students. Today's students have experienced a Web 2.0 takeover in their personal lives through blogs, wilds, podcasts, social networks, and instant messaging (Johnson, 2009).There are lots of benefits of using Web 2.0 tools. Richardson (2006) listed four things that blogging allows students to do: *(1) reflect on what they are writing and thinking as they write and think it; (2) carry on writing about a topic over a sustained period of time; (3) engage readers and audience in a sustained conversation that leads to further thinking and writing; and (4) synthesize disparate learning experiences and understand their collective relationship and relevance.*

> *"Web tools take important place in school education and in group projects.Students could also collaborate on group projects using bookmarking sites, sharing links, and uploading resources discovered, while educators could follow their students bookmark pages to gain insight on their research process and progress" (Alexander, 2006). Conole et al. (2006) note that "The increasing use of user-generated content in the form of sites such as Wikipedia is challenging the traditional norms of the academic institutions as the key knowledge expert and providers. Teachers and learners can build up collections of resources, and with a little ingenuity can also use social bookmarking systems to bookmark resources that are not on the web."Prior to wikis, blogs, social bookmarking, and social networking, there were listservs, groupware, and web-based communities linking people with common interests" (Alexander, 2006).*

Web 2.0 tools make collaboration easier than ever and they can save time and avoid duplication of effort. Many studies in the past have shown that Web 2.0 use in the classroom has increased over the past years; however, *"this use has been primarily limited to content delivery, such as accessing course materials"* (Maloney, 2007). Hewitt and Forte (2006) found that one third of the student population did not believe faculty should be on Facebook, in Georgia Institute of Technology. Lenhart and Madden (2007) said that: "More than 55% of all online American youths ages 12–17 use online social networking sites". *"The majority of studies have been comparative in nature and have focused primarily on social networking tools, such as Facebook and MySpace and their uses in many extracurricular educational contexts"* (Pence, 2007). *"The blooming of online social networks to exchange personal information, photos, videos (Facebook, Flickr, YouTube), and the increased need for tools to quickly create, analyze, and exchange the ever increasing amount of information, along with the ease of use of Web 2.0 collaboration software, have fuelled a surge in the emergence of Web 2.0 technologies"* (Dearstyne, 2007). *Currently, users utilize these sites to stay in touch with their friends, to make plans, make new friends, or flirt with somebody online* (Lenhart & Madden, 2007).

"Internet technologies such as e-mail, course websites, and newsgroups have added value to traditional classroom knowledge delivery and have impacted the course delivery and design in many colleges and universities" (Barnett, Keating, Harwook, & Saam, 2004). Some of the examples of Web 2.0 collaboration tools are: blogs, wikis, social networking, and social bookmarking. Wikis are useful in educational settings in that they support individualized learning, allowing for more socially defined search structures and promote collaboration through group editing and peer review" (Alexander, 2006). Among Web 2.0 tools; Wiki "takes place by assimilation or by accommodation respectively: people can extend their knowledge by simply adding new information, or they can modify their prior knowledge and create new knowledge" (Cress & Kimmerle, 2008). Blogs are "a great investment of technology and time to engage with our customers directly" as well as "an opportunity to test out how to augment employee communications" (Brookover, 2007).

"Schools and classrooms, both real and virtual, must have teachers who are equipped with technology resources and skills and who can effectively teach the necessary subject matter content while incorporating technology concepts and skills" (Unesco, 2008).Nevertheless, we must use them not only "as a tool that facilitates the storage, transmission and organization of the courses' content, without a significant difference between face to face courses and others courses supported by ICT " (Montes et al., 2006), "but also as a way to improve the quality of learning and to support the development of thought skills" (Jonassen and Yueh, 1998).

"These new technologies make sharing content among users and participants much easier than in the past and change the way documents are created, used, shared, and distributed" (Dearstyne, 2007). Web tools replace the traditional authoritative media delivery institutions with the wisdom of the technology. They are very beneficial, useful and new. Web tools were very efficient materials in the education system of the 20th century. There were many reseaches in the past and there will be many more. As technology advances, so does the accessibility of Web tools. If teachers structure their courses according to their students choices,their students may be more motivated. Thus, what are students choices and expectations? These are very important issues for an instructor.

1.2 Purpose of the study

The purpose of this study was to find Web 2.0 preferences of the students, to drive out students' experiences with Web 2.0 technologies and to find their expectations from Web 3.0 technologies. For this purpose an online questionnaire was prepared and interviews with the students were done.

2 Method

2.1 Population

The online survey on Surveymonkey.com was distributed to 350 students in high schools and 350 students in universities. 210 high school students and 231 university students have answered the questionnaire. Later, 15 high school students and 15 university students were chosen randomly for one-to-one interviews with the researchers.

2.2 Instrument

A questionnaire, consisting of 50 items, was created to capture data about students Web 2.0 tool preferences. Later, an interview questionnaire, consisting of 10 items was formed, to find students expectations from Web 3.0 technologies. In order to evaluate the items in the questionnaires, experts evaluation ($n = 17$) was wanted. Experts group from education technologist evaluated the data gathering scale both individually and collaboratively. Under the suggestions of experts, necessary corrections were done to the draft form of the questionnaires. Hence, the content validity was maintained by the help of the educational technologist experts. The scales used in the online questionnaire are: every day, 2-6 times a week, once a week, once a month and never. It includes questions like: How often do you use Facebook? How often do you use Plaxo? How often do you use Skype? The interview questionnaire included questions like: Are Web 2.0 tools necessary for education? What type of education do you prefer for learning Web 2.0 tools? What are your expectations from Web 3.0 tools?

2.3 Process of data collection

Online survey was posted on Surveymonkey.com and was distributed to two groups of students: aged 14-19 (high school students in North Cyprus) and 20-24(higher education students in North Cyprus). 210 high school students and 231 university students answered the questionnaires. Thus, 441 valid responses were collected between February 2009 and March 2009. One-to-one interviews were carried out with the 30 randomly selected students. Having explained the purpose of the research and how any replies and any data gathered were to be used, students were willing to participate to the online surveys.

2.4 Data analysis

The frequencies and percentages of the data obtained from online questionnaire and interview data were calculated. These were all used for data analysis.

3 Results

This section will be explained in two sub-sections: Questionnaire Results and Interview Results.

3.1 Questionnaire results

3.1.1 Why do you use Web 2.0 tools?

According to the online questionnaire results: 190 high school students said "To Communicate with friends", 210 high school students said "To communicate with my family", and 100 high school students said "For other reasons". 231 university students said "To Communicate with friends", 135 university students said "To communicate with my family", and 50 university students said "For other reasons" (See Figure 1).

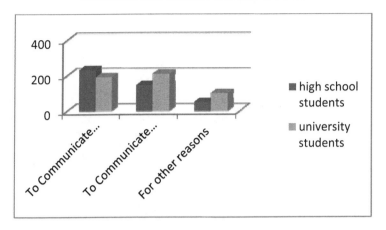

Figure 1: Reasons of using Web 2.0 tools

According to the research results, most students were using Facebook and Hi5 to communicate with their peers. Not many students surveyed were using Wikipedia, LinkedIn, and YouTube for educational purposes. Some of the interesting student answers were: Web 3.0 tools should support "multi-touch screen properties"; and Web 3.0 tools should contain "Multi-language support". Despite most of the students wanting to learn Web 2.0 tools, they said their parents and teachers do not allow them to use web tools because they think "Web 2.0 tools are waste of time".

3.1.2 Frequencies of Web 2.0 tools usages

Important online questionnaire results were: Students use Facebook 2-6 times a week (63.8%). They use Hi5 (77.5%), MySpace (75.4%), YouTube (69%), Plaxo (63%), Ning (54.9%), del.icio.us (53.1) once a week. On the other hand, they use Flixter (74.9%), Twitter (74.9) and Weblogs (52.6%) once a month (See Figure 2). However, they use the following web tools rarely: Clorblender, Yourminis, Netvibes, Viadeo, Orkut, Farecast, istat, Friendster, Vox, Tagged, Videopods, Xing, Skyrock, del.icio.us, Metacafe, Studivz, Audiopods, BlogCatolog, Furl, Lulu, Cairgslist, wufoo, cyworld, omnidrive, docstoc, standoutjobs, upcomings and pipes; with the user percentages lower than 10% The first 20 results were given in Table 1.

Table 1: Students Web 2.0 preferences

Web 2.0	Everyday	2-6 Times a Week	Once a Week	Once a Month	Never
Audiopods	0,00%	11,10%	53,10%	12,90%	22,90%
Cyworld	0,70%	0,00%	0,20%	13,30%	85,80%
del.icio.us	0,00%	11,10%	53,10%	12,90%	22,90%
Facebook	23,70%	63,80%	6,10%	3,80%	2,60%
Flixter	0,20%	0,00%	4,10%	74,90%	20,80%
Hi5	2,10%	4,40%	77,50%	4,60%	11,40%
Linkedin	3,50%	11,90%	10,70%	0,70%	73,20%
MySpace	0,70%	2,30%	75,40%	5,90%	15,70%
Netlog	0,20%	1,10%	8,90%	75,10%	14,60%
Ning	30,40%	5,90%	54,90%	7,00%	1,80%
Orkut	0,20%	0,00%	11,60%	7,00%	81,20%
Plaxo	0,50%	0,00%	63,00%	15,30%	21,20%
Tagged	0,70%	0,20%	3,50%	3,30%	92,20%
Twitter	0,20%	0,00%	4,10%	74,90%	20,80%
Viadeo	0,50%	0,00%	0,50%	17,80%	81,30%
Videopods	2,10%	4,40%	77,50%	4,60%	11,40%
Vikipedi	0,20%	0,00%	4,10%	74,90%	20,80%
Webblogs	0,20%	0,00%	5,90%	52,60%	41,20%
Xing	0,50%	0,30%	2,30%	5,90%	91,00%
Youtube	9%	16%	69%	3,50%	2,50%

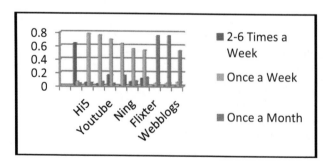

Figure 2: Frequencies of Web 2.0 tools usages

3.1.3   Are web tools useful?

When the question "What do you think about using Web 2.0/Web 3.0 tools?" is asked, high school students and university students gave different answers (See figure 3): 50 of the high school students said that "They are useful", 91 of the high school students said that "they are neither useful nor useless", 55 of them said that "Web 2.0 tools are useless" and 50 of them said that "I have not used them before, so I have no idea". On the other hand, 50 of the university students said that "They are useful", 70 of them said that "they are neither useful nor useless", 67 of them said that "They are useless", 23 of them said that "I have not used them before, so I have no idea".

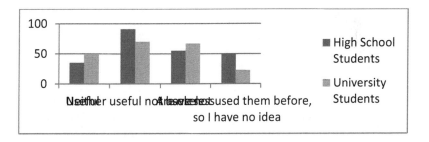

Figure 3: SurveyMonkey results: Usage of Web 2.0/Web 3.0 tools

3.1.4   Best education type for web tools
High school students answers and university school students answers to the question "Which of the following would you prefer to get more information about web 2.0 tools? (Distance Education, Traditional Education, Blended Education and Self Learning)" were similar. The total responses are as the following: Blended Education (63.7%); Self Learning (22.3%), Distance Education (8.1%) and Traditional Education (8.1%). The results can be seen in Figure 4. According to these results students' major choice of education for Web tools is Blended Education.

51. Which of the following would you prefer in order to get more information about Web 2.0 tools?		Response Percent	Response Count
Distance Education		8.1%	35
Traditional Education		5.8%	25
Blended Education		63.7%	274
Self Learning		22.3%	96
		answered question	430
		skipped question	11

Figure 4: SurveyMonkey results: which type of education?

3.2   Interview results

Many students engage with Web 2.0 technologies on a daily basis, they view them as merely social networking tools and they have much more expectations from WEB 3.0 tools. *"This shift in the role of the WWW, and of communication on it, is characterized as the shift from Web 1.0 to Web 2.0"* (Downes 2005; O'Reilly 2005), and, correspondingly, the technological tools that enable the shift are designated Web 2.0-technologies. A shift from Web 2.0 to Web 3.0 should follow. Students problems with Web 2.0 tools and their expectations from Web 3.0 tools were asked.

3.2.1   Problems with Web 2.0 tools

In the interviews carried by the researchers, students have expressed that they have 3 types of problems:

1.   "Teachers not using Web 2.0 tools"

10 out of 30 interviewed students said that: "Our Teachers are not using Web 2.0 tools". Students think this is because of the following: "They do not believe the benefits of the Web 2.0 tools"; "They think Web 2.0 tools are waste of time."; "They do not have access to Internet" and "They do not have computers in class".

2.   Not many Web 2.0 tools support Turkish language"

28 out of 30 students in the interviews said that: "Not many Web 2.0 tools support Turkish language, and we feel sad about this"

134

3. "Parents Restriction"

15 out of 30 students said that: "Our Parents restrict us since they think we shouldn't use Web 2.0 tools because they think Web 2.0 tools are waste of time".

3.2.2 Expectations from Web 3.0 tools

The students answers to the question "What are your expectations from Web 3.0 tools?" were very interesting: Different students from different schools give different answers to this question. The most common Web 3.0 expectations of the students are the following:

1. More Entertaining

% 30 of the students said that "Web 2.0 tools are boring, they should be more entertaining and more playfull".

2. More Controlable

%40 of the students said that: "We do not have much control on the tools, we should have more access on their features".

3. Multilanguage Support

%60 of the students said that: " Web 2.0 tools do not have multilanguage properties, we are having difficulties with the language","If Web tools were in Turkish language, we would have felt ourselves more comfortable and more happy".

4. Better Group Meeting Audio System

%60 of the students said that: "Web tools should have good group meeting audio system".

5. Intelligent Educational Materials

%60 of the students said that: "Web tools should contain, intelligent educational materials"

6. Compatable with Mobile Technologies

%35 of the students said that: "Web tools should be used with the mobile technologies"

7. Multi-touch Screen Properties

%10 of the students said that: "Web 3.0 tools should contain multi-touch screen properties".

4 Implications and conclusions

Many interesting results are obtained by "letting the students talk". Students who have answered the questionnaires said that: "Some teachers do not know how to use Web 2.0 tools. Some teachers know how to do not use, but they do not use Web 2.0 tools during lessons". Parents and teachers should be informed about web tools. Educators should rethink and analyze their Web 2.0/Web 3.0 choices for their courses. In their choices, they should ask their students choices. *"The use of Web 2.0 technologies in learning and teaching is considerable but patchy"* (Hughes, 2009).

What training do teachers need to be able to provide the necessary support to students using Web 2.0 tools? What motivates students to use these technologies or not to use, for which tasks they want to use them? If the lecturer is monitoring the web tools and is continuously interacting with students by giving feedback and comments on their web tools, then the students are more likely to continue using the web tool. If the lecturer is not monitoring who is writing on the web tools then students will not use it. This research study was very helpful for reshaping researcher's ideas about a "parent-teacher-student Web 3.0 portal". It's sure that with more web tool knowledge, every teacher could be better structured, resourced and organized to support more effective classroom teaching; and parents would be more willing to let their children to learn web tools.

5 Recommendations

As a result of this research study; researchers come up with some useful recommendations:

1. Organization of seminars to inform parents and teachers about the benefits of Web 2.0/Web 3.0 tools in education.
2. Develop projects together with the universities and actively monitor practice and law over control of content in a Web 2.0/Web 3.0 environment, and update their policies accordingly.

3. Develop projects, investigating how institutional repositories can be made more accessible for learning and teaching through the use of Web 2.0 and Web 3.0 technologies.
4. In order to make Web tools more widespread; multilanguage support of these tools should be provided.

6 Suggestions for further studies

The limitations of this study are restricted with high school students and university students in North Cyprus and with those whom researchers were able to contact and send email to fill the questionnaires. The following topics were suggested for further research studies:

1. What is the nature of a WEB 3.0 environment?
2. Is Semantic Web, a Web 3.0?
3. What is the best training program for fulfilling the teachers and parents "Web tool training needs"?

Further studies of the researchers would also include "Teachers Web 2.0 choices"

References

Alexander, 2006 B. Alexander, "A New Way Of Innovation For Teaching And Learning", *Educause Review 41*. Vol 2., pp. 32–44.

Brookover, S. (2007) "Why we Blog?" *Library Journal*, Vol *32*, No.19,pp. 28-31.

Cho, A. (2008).*What is Web 3.0? The Next Generation Web: Search Context for Online Informa-tion*.[online].http://internet.suite101.com/article.cfm/what_is_web_30#ixzz 0Gk3ui6Du&B

Conole, G., de Laat, M., Dillon, T., & Darby, J. (2006). *JISC LXP: "Student Experience of Technologies:Final report report"*. [Online]. http://www.jisc.ac.uk/whatwedo/programmes/elearning_pedagogy/elp_le arneroutcomes.aspx

Cress, U., & Kimmerle, J. (2008) "A Systemic and Cognitive View On Collaborative Knowledge Building With Wikis". *International Journal Of Computer-Supported Collaborative Learning,*Vol *3*. No: 2, pp.105–122.

Dearstyne, (2007) "Blogs, Mashups, and Wikis: Oh My!", *Information Management Journal* Vol 41. No: 4, pp. 24–33.

Downes, S.(2005) "E-Learning 2.0", eLearn Magazine, Vol. 2005, No.10, p.1

Giusini,D.(2006) "How Web 2.0 is Changing Medicine"Editorials. BMJ 2006;333:1283-1284, DOI:10.1136/bmj.39062.555405.80.

Hewitt, A. and Forte, A. (2006) "Crossing Boundaries: Identity Management and Student/Faculty Relationships on the Facebook", *Computer Supported Cooperative Work*, pp. 4-8.

Johnson, M. (2009), "Primary Sources and Web 2.0: Unlikely Match or Made for Each Other?" [Online], *Library Media Connection*, http://library.neu.edu.tr:2063/ehost/pdf?vid=6&hid=102&sid=ef863e62-3af8-4f0e-bce1-7d870e10921a%40sessionmgr103.

Lenhart, A., & Madden, M. (2007) *Social Networking Websites And Teens: An Overview*. Pew [online],http://www.pewinternet.org/PPF/r/198/report_display.asp.

Huges, M.(2009).Higher Education in Web 2.0 world. Report of an independent Committee of Inquiry into the impact on higher education of students' widespread use of Web 2.0 technologies Internet And American Life Project Report",

Maloney, E.(2007), "What Web 2.0 Can Teach Us About Learning", *Chronicle Of Higher Education* Vol 25. No.18, p. B26.

MacManus, R. (2007) Eric Schmidt Defines Web 3.0, [online], http://www.readwriteweb.com/archives/eric_schmidt_defines_web_30.php.

Madden,M. and Fox,S. (2006) "Riding the Waves of Web 2.0. More Than a Buzzword, But Still Not Easily Defined", Pew Internet Project,[online], http://www.co-bw.com/ethics_Web_2.pdf

Montes González, J., Solanlly Ochoa, A. (2006) "Apropiación De Las Tecnologías De La İnformación Comunicación En Cursos Universitarios", Acta Colombiana de Psicología Vol.9, No.2, pp. 87-100.

O'Reilly, T. (2005) *What Is Web 2.0: Design Patterns and Business Models for the Next Generation of Software"* [online], http://oreillynet.com/pub/a/oreilly/tim/news/2005/09/30/what-is-web-20.html.

Pence, H.E.(2007). "Preparing For The Real Web Generation", *Journal Of Educational Technology Systems*, Vol. 35, No.3, pp. 347–356.

Pew Internet and American Life Project. (2007). *"Social Networking Websites And Teens"* [online], http://www.pewinternet.org/PPF/r/198/report_display.asp.

Richardson, W. (2006) *"Blogs, Wikis, Podcasts, and Other Powerful Web Tools For Classrooms"*, Thousand Oaks,Corwin Press.

Todd, L. (2009) "What is Web 3.0 Definition?"[online] http://www.tourismkeys.ca/blog/2009/01/what-is-web-30-definition/

Unesco, (2008) *"ICT Competency Standards For Teachers"*, Paris: United Nations Educational, Scientific And Cultural Organization, [online], http://Cst.Unescoci.

Web 2.0 as a Catalyst for Rethinking Teaching and Learning in Tertiary Education: A Case Study of KDU College (Malaysia)

Alwyn Lau
KDU College, Kuala Lumpur, Malaysia
Originally published in the Proceedings of ICEL 2010

Editorial Commentary
This paper highlights some key findings and looks at some Web 2.0 trends in tertiary education in Malaysia. Amongst the highlights of the author's findings is the interesting fact that teaching staff did not attach a huge importance to the Web as a source of rethinking learning though they go on to add that all departments were positive about the implications of the Web for tertiary education. Personally, I think that Web 2.0 has huge implications for education at all levels. With the recent announcement of the MITx online learning initiative and the advent of flip-teaching that heralds the death of the traditional lecture style format of teaching, we are seeing the beginning of some remarkable changes in education.

Abstract: Web 2.0 is the wave of Internet usage characterized by collaborative sharing, blogging, real-time journaling and other media applications broadly lumped under the heading of 'social networking media'. It signals a move away from the Internet as a mere collection of computers passively sharing information to seeing the Web as an active emergent network of people who are enabled to not only interact more closely but to collaboratively shape and create new realities. This paper first outlines five trends impacting education as a result of the Web 2.0 phenomenon which educational institutions cannot ignore (connectivism, digital creation, collaboration, divergent assessment and open courseware) then shares the research performed on faculty (incl. management) and students of KDU College (based in Petaling Jaya), the first college in Malaysia to implement an e-forum for the Malaysian Ministry of Higher Education's compulsory subjects. The research sought to answer questions relating to the benefits and/or challenges which Web 2.0 have brought to teaching and learning, the extent to which the five characteristics have impacted the students, lecturers and management and future issues anticipated. This paper will highlight some key findings and attempt a generalization of Web 2.0 trends to tertiary education in Malaysia and recommend broad action-steps forward, both in the national context as well as the global one.

Keywords: Web 2.0, eLearning, open learning, assessment, connectivism, education, collaboration

1   Web 2.0 (an introduction)

Web 2.0 is the wave of Internet usage characterized by collaborative sharing, blogging, real-time journaling and other media applications broadly lumped under the heading of 'social networking media'. These applications would include the popular tools and websites like Facebook, MySpace, Linked-In and Bebo, all of which are (understandably fuzzy) expressions of the move towards the creation of online communities and networks which harness the collective intelligence (O'Reilly, 2006).

Web 1.0, being the first 'wave' of Internet familiarity and usage, focused on what individuals can do online qua individuals. These common tasks would include downloading files, creating a (usually static) Web presence in the form of personal websites, viewing and listing information and browsing in general. Web 2.0 signals a move away from the Internet as a mere collection of computers passively sharing information to seeing the Web as an active emergent network of people who are enabled to not only interact more closely but to collaboratively shape and create new realities. From the initial emphasis of consuming what was 'out there', now surfers are acting as 'pro-sumers' who use and share objects and cyber-goods for their own use and satisfaction.

Drumgoole (2006), in true intuitive Web 2.0 fashion, writes in his blog that: "Web 1.0 was about *companies*, Web 2.0 is about *communities*...Web 1.0 was about *wires*, Web 2.0 is about *wireless*...Web 1.0 was about *owning*, Web 2.0 is about *sharing*... Web 1.0 is about web *forms*, Web 2.0 is about web *applications*... Web 1.0 was about *hardware* costs, Web 2.0 is about *bandwidth* costs."

In a word, Web 2.0 is a new *state of mind* (Heuer, 2006) on how to be, behave and engage with the global Web community.

Web 2.0 in education is a sub-component of the more generic term, eLearning, in that the latter involves any and every use of the World Wide Web for educational purposes. Bates (2004) notes that since 1995 when the World Wide Web emerged, online universities have bloomed ranging from public and private partnerships to national and international consortia to the creation of virtual schools.

However, eLearning prior to Web 2.0 involves primarily *supplementing* traditional pedagogical modes with an online component (e.g. clicking on the correct answers, obtaining educational materials online) whereas social networking encourages a more constructivist approach which makes deeper use of reflection and discussion, and in which educational design is reconsidered (e.g. e-forums, collaborative learning, problem-based learning, etc.).

2 Five trends in Web 2.0 and education (a literature review)

This essay will first outline five trends impacting education as a result of the Web 2.0 phenomenon. It will argue that Web 2.0 has and will continue to transform eLearning such that educational institutions (and pedagogical thinking) will be unable to ignore the emergence of the below characteristics

2.1 Connectivism

This is a theory of learning which acknowledges to the extent to which the learner has connected (digitally) with learners (incl. non-human ones) with divergent views. Developed by George Siemens (2005), connectivism pulls together our understanding of learning with and 'into' the Web, making the former inseparable from a continually productive use of the latter.

Often contrasted with other learning theories like behaviourism, cognitivism and constructivism, connectivism is the latest (re)definition of what learning *is*. This question is undeniably significant in a world where computers and the Internet have become ubiquitous and whole economies rely on them. No longer, argues writers like Siemens, can learning be understood as the mere replication of observable behaviour (i.e. behaviourism), the coding, manipulation and re-presentation of information (i.e. cognitivism) or even the creative design and building of new objects or meaning (i.e. constructivism).

Learning cannot be fully understood apart from the phenomenon of forming connections. Too much complexity has emerged in the world such that *competence* and *mastery* must be seen as a function of being linked to divergent networks, non-human sources and interactive nodes; of being able to 'see' new connections and to distinguish significant from non-significant ones; of making sound decisions about one's learning (as an act of learning itself); even, especially in the context of Web 2.0, of being able to "store one's knowledge in one's friends" i.e. the understanding that one's learning grows together with one's number of contacts/friends (see Stephenson).

The principles of connectivism are summarized (Siemens, 2005) as per below (emphasis added):

- Learning and knowledge rests in diversity of opinions and is a process of connecting specialized nodes or information sources; nurturing and maintaining connections is needed to facilitate continual learning; the ability to see connections between fields, ideas, and concepts is a core skill.
- Learning may reside in non-human appliances and currency (accurate, up-to-date knowledge) is the intent of all connectivist learning activities.
- Capacity to know more is more critical than what is currently known
- Decision-making is itself a learning process. Choosing what to learn and the meaning of incoming information is seen through the lens of a shifting reality. While there is a right answer now, it may be wrong tomorrow due to alterations in the information climate affecting the decision.

It is easy to see how the theory forms and is formed by Web 2.0 trends. More and more students are using the Internet as part of their everyday lives, and more and more of them are less and less satisfied with being passive users. Real-time connection, autonomy, total flexibility, continual creation and instant updating are the norms of Web life. Flew (2004) has noted the ways the Internet has evolved from the 1990s' onwards, one of which is how the Web is much more, "integrated into the everyday activities of individuals, the conduct of organizations, and the pursuit of commercial activity."

If the act of being alive is becoming virtually (pun intended) synonymous with being connected (in more vigorous and creative ways), then the act of learning cannot be grasped as if connections were of low importance. This follows on the idea that the act of *working* can no longer remain the same, having been transformed by what Manuel Castells terms the 'network society' which has begotten a new economy which depends, "on innovation as the source of productivity growth, on computer-networked global financial markets, whose criteria for valuation are influenced by information turbulences, on the networking of production and management, internally and externally, locally and globally, and on labor that is flexible and adaptable in all cases." (Castells, 2004)

If this is right, then problems will abound for educators and educational institutions who have not yet made the shift to a connectivist mind-set; lecturers and colleges still promoting roteLearning or failing to incorporate cyber-oriented concepts as a central feature of their teaching are certain to encounter student problems such as boredom, inattention, non-enthusiasm and difficulties linked to differences in a central understanding of what it means to learn.

2.2 Digital creation, collaboration and divergent assessment

A strong corollary of connectivism is that learning outcomes must include a digital-cyber component i.e. digital literacy in the form of technological constructivism and creation becomes a non-negotiable and students (and, most importantly, lecturers!) must be taught to build digital objects *as part of* their learning.

If we are to avoid the destructive disjuncture between students who navigate informally in Web 2.0 contexts but are required to undergo formal instruction in Web 1.0 environments (Lankshear & Knobel, 2005), schools and colleges must build encourage both students and educators to move *higher up* along Bloom's digital taxonomy (Churches, 2009), itself based on the revision to Bloom's taxonomy (Anderson & Krathwohl, 2001).

Again, this is not about just switching from traditional media to cyber-media; it's about redesigning what learning involves and is all about. Educational syllabi, 'task-sheets', homework and other learning activities – to be consistent with the tenets of connectivism – must be tied in and insepa-rable from the goal of nurturing Web 2.0 literacy. Digital-literacy skills (e.g. blogging, podcasting, etc.) ought to be considered as important (if not more so) than information-literacy skills (e.g. referencing, citation, etc.), without rejecting the latter.

Bloom's (or Churches') *digital* taxonomy (see Appendix B) also exposes a potentially gaping divide between the higher-order digital skills that the younger generation of students possess and the lower-order ones which the older generation of educators are as yet struggling with(!).

Given this divide, it becomes imperative for educators to ensure that skills like animating, broadcasting, media-clipping and so on are not confined to I.T.- or media-related courses but included even into Business and Social Science courses like Literature, History and Management. Not least also educational institutions would have to begin inserting digital literacy (and even mastery?) as a key criteria for faculty selection, appraisal and promo-tion.

Lecturer training and induction programs (both in-house and externally sourced) must include the Web 2.0 component. KDU College, in fact, began introducing '21st century learning' as part of its 3-month long faculty induc-tion program and also its delivery of the Cambridge International Diploma for Teachers & Trainers (CIDTT) program; many of the participants of this research are ex-students in these two courses.

Next, if Web 2.0, digital literacy and the new learning network paradigms (Albors, Ramos & Hervas 2008) are to be embedded into education, this would render virtually obsolete the idea of the lone learner. Thus, another effect of Web 2.0 is that learning outcomes must include teamwork and collaborative projects, a not entirely unfamiliar trajectory given the rise of multiple-intelligence paradigms emphasizing inter-personal kinds of smart (Gardner, 1993), studies (e.g. by Ward, 2009) which suggests that students' motivation (at least in the case of classroom writing) may *increase* if they're writing to be reviewed by peers or even external professionals and even calls to prioritize collaboration for the sake of human survival (Goerner, 2007).

Collaboration, simply put, is 'two or more' learners working together on a project, assignment or piece of course material with the objective of producing results they couldn't yield alone. It has reaped profound rewards and opened up previously unimaginable opportunities for businesses and for the redrawing of value-boundaries and knowledge objects (Tapscott & Williams, 2006).

Social networking media then is essentially one huge collaborative phenomenon and – risks of 'bad collaboration' (which is worse than no collaboration) aside (see Hansen, 2009) – if learning is to keep in step with Web-based progress, educators and students alike will have to learn how to connect, work and even 'play' well with others, especially in an age where face-to-face meetings are increasingly rare (despite their benefits, see Young 2008) and team members are ad-hoc, impermanent and relate *only* online. Collaboration as a learning (and assessment) activity promotes the all-too-necessary interpersonal element in personal development and knowledge construction, an often neglected element in academia, as reflected in the continued rejection of Wikipedia as an accepted academic reference despite (or because of) its reflection of 'social knowing' i.e. the idea that knowledge is best shaped through a collaborative conversation and not in an ivory tower (Weinberger, 2007).

It was in the spirit of collaborative learning that KDU College, on the suggestion of this writer, became the first educational institution in Malaysia to launch an e-forum for the Ministry of Higher Education (MOHE)'s compulsory subjects or, in Malay, *Mata Pelajaran Wajib* (MPW). The forum enables students reading Malaysian Studies, Moral Studies and Islamic Studies – the three MPW subjects – to experience 8 weeks (more than half of the 14-weeks allocated per subject) of interactive learning. (See Appendix A for screen-shots of the forum)

Given the changes to learning activities and even the priorities of education, it is only natural to question the means and methods of assessment.

Web 2.0 should pave the way for more peer-to-peer assessments, real-world problem-based work and cyber-oriented tests of student perform-ance (not to mention lecturer-appraisals).

Furthermore, if learning will take place more and more outside traditional classrooms and will involve establishing rich connections to diverse re-sources and other people (Lankshear & Knobel, 2006) it is only logical that assessments follow suit.

2.3   Open courseware

From an institutional perspective, the uploading of free educational mate-rial by colleges and universities appears to be imminent and is already made popular by universities like Massachusetts Institute of Technology (M.I.T.) (Thomas, 2007), University of Queensland, etc. In Malaysia, how-ever, open courseware remains a rarity and thus a strong marketing inno-vation option.

The growing availability of open courseware would, however, be simply a matter of time in a century which has seen shifts in the value of knowledge from its relative *scarcity* to the speed and creativity with which people *share* and *use* knowledge which is free. Nowadays, amateur investigators in almost any field enjoy better facilities for free research and analysis than full-time professionals could buy in previous decades." (Coffee, 2001).

The phenomenon of academic material given free of charge to anyone who can get connected to the Internet is but one more expression of a shift to a culture where value resides in and is created by sharing, networking and collaboration. In this new world, educational institutions who insist of re-maining closely protective of and obsessed with 'intellectual property rights' (manifested in, say, a great fear that competitors might steal their work) would not be merely missing the point but also missing out on the competitive edge(s) afforded by Web 2.0

Interestingly enough, at the time of writing, no educational institution in Malaysia has carved out a marketing or strategic position via the use of open courseware.

3 Research on KDU College

3.1 Structure, strategy and limitations

Qualitative research was performed on selected faculty (incl. management) and students of KDU College (based in Petaling Jaya, Selangor, Malaysia), which has recently had the honour of being the first college in Malaysia to implement an e-forum for the Malaysian Ministry of Higher Education's (MOHE) *Mata Pelajaran Wajib* (MPW) i.e. mandatory subjects for all pre-university students. The college has also gradually been introduced, via the author's role in its Teaching & Learning Center, to blogging as a learning and assessment tool, not to mention Web 2.0 as a whole. Questionnaires and interviews were used to compile data in an attempt to answer the following questions related to KDU College:

- What benefits and/or challenges have been encountered as a result of the introduction of Web 2.0 applications into teaching and learning?
- To what extent has the e-forum changed the teaching and learning of the MOHE's compulsory subjects?
- To what extent has blogging and other Web 2.0 applications transformed the way lecturers facilitate classes and the way students learn?
- To what extent are the (above) five characteristics of Web 2.0 evident in the college and what issues (strategic, executional, etc.) are being faced or anticipated?
- How should the college as an educational institution in Malaysia act with respect to Web 2.0? What are some future steps foreseen?

The sample participants consisted of 30 staff members of KDU College and 23 students. The questions posed were generally simple with at most four distinctions in attitudes. The limited flexibility is necessary to obtain a more definite, if rather broad, categorization of results. I have also designed the questionnaire in such a way as to 'force' either a positive or negative response (i.e. all contained an *even* number of alternatives) so as to avoid the fence-sitting I feel is very common among Malaysian respondents.

This research was limited in scope by the following factors:

- The focus is only on tertiary education
- The focus is only on one educational institution in Malaysia: KDU College, a private institution offering pre-university diplomas, certificates and external programs with institutions from Australia, United Kingdom, Switzerland, etc.
- Departments within the college vary in size (e.g. less than half a dozen lecturers for Law but about twenty for Hotel) hence the relevance and applicability of the data could be uneven (both across departments and certainly in any attempt to generalize to the Malaysian industry as a whole)

3.2 Highlights of key findings

Generally, it is unsurprising that overall students were more familiar with Web 2.0 applications than staff. Among faculty, the Mass Communication and Business departments were clearly the more frequent and familiar uses of Web technology and Bloom's digital taxonomy (both scored the highest in the first two categories). Remarkably, the Engineering department scored the lowest overall and is clearly the least responsive to Web 2.0 initiatives and potential. Interestingly enough, one of the items the students ranked highest – fresh applications for learning – is also the item the staff ranked lowest(!). Could this reflect a greater eagerness of the younger generation of learners for novelty in learning and/or a reluctance on the part of academics to change how they teach? Quite strikingly, the staff too did *not* attach overtly huge relevance/importance to the Web as a source of rethinking learning(!). It could be said that all the departments are positive about the implications of Web for tertiary education. Notable low-scores were the Hotel school regarding the Web *as a source of fresh learning* applications and the Engineering school on the Web *as a tracking/assessment instrument*. With the Hotel school this may be expected given the very experience-oriented nature of the hotel and tourism industry – as yet there is no such thing as taking a vacation online. As for why Engineering faculty may not be keen on Web-tracking students' work, one explanation could be the nature of the assessments which usually involves working with electronic equipment, machines, their circuitry, etc.

The results of the management mirror tended to mirror those of the Hotel school (and the Staff's response), in that they were relatively unenthusiastic about new online learning applications. This is a rich item to explore as it raises many questions, e.g.:

- Why a low score here when the other categories scored relatively high?
- Were the high scores in the other areas due to the subjective, vague and abstract nature of the issues (e.g. 'rethinking learning', 'participatory learning'), whereas online applications have a definite (albeit virtual) element to it i.e. if the program hasn't been seen yet, then it's best not to be welcoming of it?

The staff was most positive about *collaboration* as a key factor in education, suggesting an openness to non-individualistic forms of learning. This resonates well with the above-par interest in rethinking assessments and the use of the Web in encouraging participatory learning. It is disappointing, however, to note that the overall staff response to *blogging* as a means of facilitating learning isn't enthusiastic. Among the departments, some notable disinterest included the Pre-University department's take on global connectedness as a definition of learning. The Law department also appeared less than fully interested with embedding a cyber-component into the syllabus and providing free materials online.

3.3 Analysis and recommendations

It needs to be stated from the start that, regardless of occasional concerns and lack of interest, overall both students and staff of KDU College have demonstrated a clearly *positive* attitude towards the Web and Web 2.0 as an instrument for the processing and performance of teaching and learning. If the college is at all representative of the Malaysian tertiary education, then the results would indicate much potential in this direction. The results at least on the surface suggest that those who have a *higher* propensity to view Web 2.0 as an educationally-transforming phenomenon are also:

- Those who spend more time online
- Those who are more familiar with social media applications
- Those with a lower academic qualification (in this case, Bachelor's degree and below)

- Those who've worked for fewer years in education (in this case, less than 10 years)

Without extrapolating too strongly, based on the survey we could make the following recommendations to better nurture Web 2.0 into the spirit and operations of learning institutions in Malaysia:

- The *Media & Mass Communication* departments should **lead the way in embracing Web 2.0** given the greater openness of the faculty to innovative forms of learning and the constant engagement with new media (which is almost by definition what Web 2.0 is). Given the culturally introspective nature of this area of studies and how difficult it is to draw the line between new media as syllabus, as learning activity and as cultural environment, the departments' students and faculty could be perfectly poised to spear-head projects and events which inform, instruct and infuse Web 2.0 into the consciousness of the organization. At this point, it is important to note that a kind of organizational 'action learning' (Rogers, 2007) may be required before productive implementation of Web 2.0 is witnessed.

- The *Pre-University* departments, should educational institutions have one, are also a community well-suited to **support experimentation and development in integrating higher learning with the latest in online social media and technology.** The comparatively less complex and more flexible syllabus may allow greater fluidity in using Web 2.0 applications (although the lesser-trained and generally less exposed students could work against this idea). Nevertheless, the relatively 'shocking' lack of change stimulated by blogging is a key area to address and if nothing else highlights the critical nature of implementation i.e. people may *say* they have a strong interest in something but unless their eventual (and on-going) experience with the item is productive, positive change might be slow in forthcoming.

- Disciplines which are skill-based, hands-on and which conventionally are *not* drawn towards emerging media (e.g. *Engineering, Hotel and Languages*) will need **longer preparation cum 'incubation' time before Web 2.0 is fully accepted**; and whilst it'd be certainly unwise to focus Web 2.0-related path-breaking efforts here, it may help to construct ways in which Web 2.0 applications may be

150

embedded as part of the syllabus. This is to say that, given (what could be) a natural disinclination towards Web 2.0, students and faculty may have to experience its full-blown benefits before being willing to take further steps.

- From the perspective of specific faculty members, without at all alienating the more senior lecturers and professors, the results imply that revitalizing education with Web 2.0 may be an **endeavor best led by the junior members of staff and/or those with fewer years in education**.

- From the perspective of the *students*, it may be prudent to **not introduce overly unfamiliar assessment techniques until a later phase**. This is to avoid the anxiety normally associated with passing and excelling in examinations and/or to help ease the transition to new forms of *testing* by first ensuring that students are accustomed to new forms of *learning*.

It must be duly noted that should an educational institution seriously embark on a Web 2.0 mega-project, there will be a need to manage the potential political backlash resulting from various departments and even 'classes' of faculty taking the front-seat. Nobody ever said change was easy.

4 Conclusion

Bill Gates, founder of Microsoft, once said that the Internet is the town square of the global village that is our world of tomorrow. If education is to play a key role in shaping the thinking and direction of this global village, this entails that schools and colleges have to do serious business with the Web and all that it offers and represents. The phenomenon of Web 2.0 is an advent promising transformation for educational institutions willing and able to take bold steps to devise empowering faculty- and student- combinations of experience and experimentation to take their repertoire, *modus operandi* and service-offerings forward in to the future - both real and virtual.

References

Albors, J., Ramos, J., & Hervas, J.. (2008). New learning network paradigms: Communities of objectives, crowdsourcing, wikis and open source. International Journal of Information Management, 28(3), 194. Retrieved August 16, 2009, from ABI/INFORM Global. (Document ID: 1490789221).

Anderson, L. W. and David R. Krathwohl, D. R., et al (Eds..) (2001) A Taxonomy for Learning, Teaching, and Assessing: A Revision of Bloom's Taxonomy of Educational Objectives. Allyn & Bacon. Boston, MA (Pearson Education Group)

Baldi, S., Heier, H., & Mehler-Bicher, A. (2003, September). Open Courseware and Open Source Software. Communications of the ACM, 46(9), 105-107. Retrieved August 17, 2009, from Business Source Premier database.

Castells, M. (2004) Informationalism and the network society, in Castells, M. (ed.) (2004) The network society: A cross-cultural perspective, Cheltenham:Edward Elgar Publishing Inc.d

Castells, M. (ed.) (2004) The network society: A cross-cultural perspective, Cheltenham:Edward Elgar Publishing Inc.d

Coffee, P. (2001, July 2). IT IS COMMON KNOWLEDGE. eWeek, 18(26), 41. Retrieved August 17, 2009, from Business Source Premier database.

Churches, A. Educational Origami, Wikispaces, http://edorigami.wikispaces.com/

Craig. D Changing theories of learning, Seoul National University, retrieved at Aug 10th 2009 from http://danielcraig.com/publicfolder/Changing%20Theories%20of%20Learning.doc

Dillenbourg, P. (1999) What do you mean by collaborative learning? In Dillenbourg, P. (ed) Collaborative learning: Cognitive & computational approaches, Oxford: Elsevier.

Drumgoole, J. (2006) Web 2.0 vs Web 1.0, Copacetic, retrieved Aug 19th 2009 from http://joedrumgoole.com/blog/2006/05/29/web-20-vs-web-10/

Fernando, A. (2008, March). Baby steps in Web 2.0 education. Communication World, 25(3), 8-9. Retrieved July 30, 2009, from Business Source Premier database.

Flew, T. (2004) New media: An introduction, 2nd ed. Oxford: Oxford University Press.

Fisch, K. & MacLeod, S. 'Shift Happens 3.0' (available on YouTube), join the Shift-Happens Wikispaces at http://www.shifthappens.wikispaces.com/

Gardner, H. (1993) Frames of mind: The theory of multiple intelligences, Basic Books

Goerner, S.. (2007). Today's Copernican flip: how putting collaborative learning at the hub of human evolution improves our chances of survival. Systems Research and Behavioral Science, 24(5), 481. Retrieved August 16, 2009, from ABI/INFORM Global. (Document ID: 1405147041).

Hansen, M. (2009) Collaboration: How Leaders Avoid the Traps, Create Unity, and Reap Big Results. Cambridge, Mass.: Harvard Business Press. (2009)

Hargadon, S. (2008) Web 2.0 is the future of education, retrieved on August 9th 2009 from http://www.stevehargadon.com/2008/03/web-20-is-future-of-education.html

Heuer, C. (2006) Web 2.0 is a state of mind, Chris' Insytes, retrieved Aug 18th 2009 from http://chrisheuer.blogspot.com/2006/03/web-20-is-state-of-mind.html

Lankshear, C. & Knobel, M. (2005) Digital literacies: Policy, pedagogy and research considerations for education, Opening Plenary Address to ITU Conference (Oslo, Norway), retrieved Aug 12th 2009 from http://www.geocities.com/c.lankshear/Oslo.pdf

Lankshear, C. & Knobel, M. (2006) New literacies: Everyday practices and classroom learning, Open University Press

Leteney, F.. (2009, July). No pain, no gain. E.learning Age,18. Retrieved July 30, 2009, from ABI/INFORM Global. (Document ID: 1807156511).

Meister, J. (2008, January). Three Learning Trends to Watch in 2008. Chief Learning Officer, 7(1), 54-54. Retrieved August 17, 2009, from Business Source Premier database.

NCTE Framework for 21st Century Curriculum & Assessment, NCTE (National Council of Teachers of English), retrieved Aug 18th 2009 from http://www.ncte.org/governance/21stcenturyframework

O'Reilly, T. (2006) Web 2.0 compact definition: Trying again, retrieved August 5th 2009, from http://radar.oreilly.com/archives/2006/12/web-20-compact.html

PR Newswire (2008) New Study Shows Time Spent Online Important for Teen Development. (20 November) Retrieved August 5, 2009, from ABI/INFORM Dateline. (Document ID: 1598259561).

Prensky, M. (2001) Digital Natives, On the Horizon, NCB University Press, Vol. 9 No. 5, October 2001

Rogers, J. (2007) Adults Learning, Open University Press, Mc-Graw Hill

Siemens, G. (2005) Connectivism: A Learning Theory for the Digital Age, International Journal of Instructional Technology and Distance Learning, Vol. 2 No. 1, Jan 2005

Stephenson, K. What knowledge tears apart, networks make whole, Internal Communication Focus, no.36, retrieved Aug 11th 2009 from http://www.netform.com/html/icf.pdf

Tapscott, D. & Williams, A. (2006) Wikinomics: How Mass Collaboration Changes Everything, London: Atlantic Books

Thomas, K. (2007, February). MIT puts entire curriculum at disposal of e-learners. Information World Review, Retrieved August 17, 2009, from Business Source Premier database.

Ward, M.. (2009). Squaring the Learning Circle: Cross-Classroom Collaborations and the Impact of Audience on Student Outcomes in Professional Writing. Journal of Business and Technical Communication, 23(1), 61. Retrieved August 16, 2009, from ABI/INFORM Global. (Document ID: 1603220741).

Weinberger, D. (2007) Everything is Miscellaneous: The power of the new digital disorder, Times Books

Williams, J., & Chinn, S.. (2009). Using Web 2.0 to Support the Active Learning Experience. Journal of Information Systems Education, 20(2), 165-174. Retrieved July 30, 2009, from ABI/INFORM Global. (Document ID: 1755224761).

Young, T. (2008, November). When face-to-face is the best way to collaborate. Knowledge Management Review, 11(5), 3. Retrieved August 16, 2009, from ABI/INFORM Global. (Document ID: 1605260301)

Zikmund, W. (2003) Business Research Methods, Thomson South-Western

Appendix A: KDU's eForum for the MQA's compulsory subjects (photos)

Photo 1: The Start Page

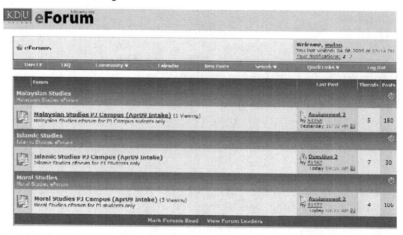

Photo 2: A Discussion Thread on Democratization

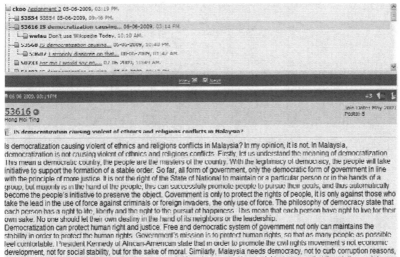

Photo 3: A Discussion Thread on Islam

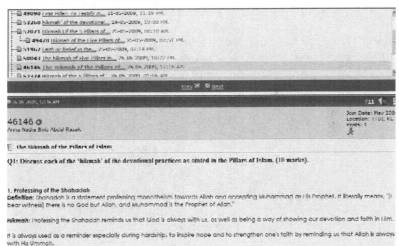

Appendix B: Bloom's digital taxonomy

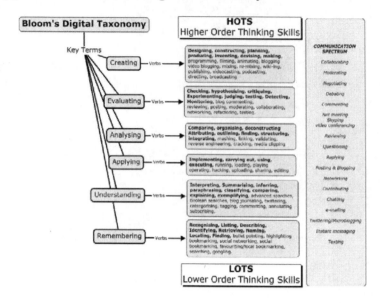

Source: Churches, A. (2009) Bloom's Digital Taxonomy, Educational Origami, Wikispaces, retrieved on Aug 11th 2009 from http://edorigami.wikispaces.com/Bloom's+Digital+Taxonomy

Social Media Networking Tools (SMNT): Concepts, Challenges and Corollaries of Organisational Work Practices

Aurilla Aurelie Bechina[1] and Eli Hustad[2]
[1]Buskerud University College, Faculty of Technology, Kongsberg, Norway
[2]University of Agder, Kristiansand, Norway

Originally published in the Proceedings of ECMLG 2011

Editorial Commentary

This conceptual paper sheds light on the concepts, opportunities and challenges of social networking in business. It gives a nice overview of Web 2.0 technologies and compares Web 1.0 with Web 2.0. It makes the point, with which I fully concur, that for Enterprise 2.0 to be successful, participants must see the value in it. It finally touches on the future of the web as a semantic web where web sites and machines can exchange information in meaningful ways. If this is dubbed Web 3.0 then let me leave you with a question. What will the future of KM look like and will there be a KM 3.0?

Abstract: During the last decade, enterprise strategists started to recognize that business success and performance improvement was more and more related to the degree to which new technological trends were used in the organisations. Indeed, the role of the information communication technologies has increased in improving the social and business life of people. Internet and Web 2.0 has brought a revolution in the way people are interacting with each others. Although that several benefits have been reported in using social network for business processes improvement; there is still a stringent need to investigate more closely the implication of using social technologies in organisational work practices. This conceptual paper based on a literature review intends to shed a light on the concepts, opportunities and challenges of social networking tools in business practices. The paper outlines a framework encompassing factors that could facilitate or hamper the adoption of the Web 2.0 technologies by organisations.

Keywords: Web 2.0, social networking, networks of practice, knowledge sharing, Enterprise2.0, Folksonomies

1   Introduction

The advances in information and communication technology (ICT) have influenced on the emergence of the contemporary networking society based upon a decentralized, information-driven and knowledge-based economy (Castells, 2000).

The evolution of Internet as a large scale information infrastructure provides opportunities for social networking where individuals take part in online communication to share information and knowledge across spatial and temporal boundaries.

Internet technologies and web-based applications are continuously developing and advancing. This innovation has caused improved usability attracting several communities to popular online activities. Individuals make new friendships differently than before by sharing personal profiles (e.g. Facebook.com), exchanging multimedia files (YouTube.com) and by taking part in virtual games (WorldofWarCraft.com). People share common interests by participating in different discussion forums and by making their own blogs. Furthermore, Wikis are increasingly used for easy creation and frequently updating of information content at web-sites (e.g. Wikipedia). People are making and sharing their own metadata in terms of social tagging and bookmarks (i.e. Folksonomies). Scholars and practitioners alike suggest that these contemporary trends of Internet development represent a paradigm shift towards the second generation of the web conceptualized as the Web 2.0 phenomenon (Musser & O'Reilly, 2006).

While Web 2.0 in terms of social networking technologies is widely applied among people within their private life for amusing purposes, for meeting new friends and for pursuing and discussing common hobbies within their leisure time, there is a still a need to further investigate whether social media could improve the organisational work practices.

The last couple of years, several research studies discussing the new trends based on the usage of social media within business context have been published (Grossman & McCarthy, 2007; Harrison & Thomas, 2009; Sau-ling, 2010). However, there are still too little investigations done on the corollaries of the usage social media technologies on organisational work practices.

This conceptual paper aims to discuss the Web 2.0 perspectives related to business context. For instance, the main principle of self organizing which social networking build upon may challenge the traditional organizational ontology in terms of structural, cultural and managerial perceptions. This paper discusses important challenges and opportunities that Web 2.0 may bring along within an organizational context.

The section two introduces the basic concepts of the social media networking technologies. The third part outlines the emerging concepts of enterprise 2.0 while the last section discusses the possible implications of Web 2.0 on the organisational work practices.

2   Web 2.0 concepts, opportunities and challenges

Web 2.0 and its related elements were introduced through a brainstorming session at a conference launched by the computer book publisher O'Reilly and the event organizer MediaLive International in 2004 (O'Reilly, 2005).

The Web 2.0 phenomenon has gained tremendous visibility and has attracted strong interests not only from the scientific community but as well from businesses and IT vendors (Smith, 2008). This has generated some conflicting definitions of Web 2.0 since IT vendors are trying to capitalize on this trend by associating their products with Web 2.0 attributes, like they did with KM technologies in the mid 90's. Web 2.0 is a controversial term, and there exists different definitions. To elaborate the ramifications from this debate, however, is beyond the scope of this paper, and we apply the following definition of Web 2.0 as introduced by Musser and O'Reilly (2006):

Web 2.0 is a set of economic, social, and technology trends that collectively form the base for the next generation of the Internet – a more mature, distinctive medium characterized by user participation, openness, and network effects.

The Web 2.0 reflects this new concept of gravitational core identified as the web as platform, user controlled data, architectures of participation, cost-effective scalability, re-mixable data source and data transmissions, and harnessing collective intelligence (Tapscott, 2006a).

Web 2.0 should be seen as the convergence of two driving trends, one technological oriented and one emphasizing social dimensions. This convergence leads to new business models with user-contributed content. The features leverage a diverse participatory intellectual capital to enhance the transparency of business processes and to distribute participatory services and products design.

In opposition to Web 1.0, users can easily generate and publish content. The second generation of the web tends to be more dynamically and user-centric in orientation compared to its first generation, Web 1.0. Indeed, typical characteristics of Web 1.0 are a less dynamic nature consisting static content published at separate websites representing information silos. In addition, the content of these earlier websites were rather predefined and only a few people were involved in the creation of this information.

Furthermore, the users are becoming so-called prosumers (Toffler, 1981), referring to a phenomenon where a customer represents both producer and consumer. Transferred to the context of Internet, it follows that a user is now both producing and consuming information at a website (Tapscott & Willams, 2006). The second generation of the web corresponds more to the original objective and vision of the Internet which did not originally differentiate between the users and creators of information since the same software was to be used to browse the web and to create new web-pages (Berners-Lee, 2000). Nor did he distinguish between internal business resources and the external web, while companies did develop and still have closed intranets.

Web 2.0 is a platform for interacting with content. Information is broken up into "micro-content" units that may be distributed across the Web. A new set of tools such as RSS (Really Simple Syndication) provide mechanisms that creates a "feed" of updates from specified news sites, blogs and so forth. RSS contributes to publishing, aggregating and combining micro-content in new and useful ways.

The table 1 summarizes central differences between Web 1.0 and Web 2.0.

Table 1: Differences between Web 1.0 and Web 2.0

Web 1.0	Web 2.0
Websites as isolated information silos	Websites as interlinked computing platforms
Static websites, download	Dynamic websites, upload and download
Content management systems	Wikis
Directories (taxonomy)	Folksonomies
Britannica Online	Wikipedia
Personal websites	Blogging
Small "content development groups"	User-created content
Publishing	Participating and building social networks
HTML, hypertext	Ajax (JavaScript, XML), mash-ups
Software created by computer experts	Users became co-creators and develop applications
Annual or more seldom releases (Microsoft)	Perpetual beta (Google) "Open source" related development

The collective intelligence of users encourages more democratic use and participation (Boulos & Wheeler, 2007). Initially, the primarily goal of the World Wide Web (WWW) was to foster a better collaboration among the scientific communities by sharing ideas and knowledge. However, it is only with the emergence of Web 2.0 technologies that we start to recognize its impacts on leveraging knowledge exchanged and enhancing business processes in organizations.

Web 2.0, could be seen as the emergence of mass collaboration (Tapscott & Willams, 2006), in which several users participate actively and thereby create mutual benefits in terms of increasing returns (Shapiro & Varian, 1999). Web 2.0 relies on network effects that cause increasing returns as a consequence of mass collaboration (Tapscott & Willams, 2006). It follows that data directories and web-sites get richer the more people interact with them. The foundation for mass collaboration is the overlapping structure of social networks that constitutes the overall Internet representing an information infrastructure of web-based communities, technologies and hosted services.

Through social networking sites, Wikis and Folksonomies the second generation of the web aims to facilitate collaboration and sharing of knowledge and best practices between users, and the web is becoming a platform for user-created content.

Thus, Web 2.0 as such represents a renaissance of the original idea – which needed to mature gradually for being implemented in practice in order to foster collaboration amongst the users.

Social software applications and tools are perceived as the outcome of the popularity and the rapid development of Web 2.0 concepts. The next part reviews the different Web 2.0 technologies.

2.1   Web 2.0 technologies

Although the term Web 2.0 implicitly symbolizes an upgrade to a new version of the World Wide Web, it does not refer to an update of technical specifications or new releases of software, but rather "the 2.0" intends to illustrate the changes in the ways software developers and end-users are *using* the web.

Typical technologies that support user-created content are: wiki's, like Wikipedia; blogging, such as Blogger; social networking such as Facebook; and social bookmarking, such as Del.Icio.Us.

Wiki comes from the Hawaiian word for fast. Wiki is a collaborative mechanism that allows people to contribute or modify content using a simplified markup language. Wiki is usually used to support the community building website. Wikipedia, an open content encyclopedia, is considered as one of the most popular examples of a wikis. Wikis allow users to enter, aggregate, and annotate content. The underlying concept lies on the collective wisdom to produce an organized, thorough, and searchable database in various domains such as political, humanitarian, education, history, and so forth. Although, security issues in organizational use of wikis Security have been tackled by putting in place some mechanisms to restrict viewing or editing content; there are still some concerns to limit the access as it against the concept of freely contribution. In addition, the quality of the content can be questionable if the self-organizing editing and vetting is not adequate.

Blogs are the most personal and controversial of the Web 2.0 applications and more especially in business contexts. Web sites can be created spontaneously and maintained by individuals making it possible to maintain an online journal on which others can comment for private use or business purpose. Hence, activities discussions can emerge from dynamic use of the Blogging feature. The biggest advantage resides in the possibility for participants to interact with others. For example, HP is encouraging its employee to use blog feature to discuss issues on printer compatibility with customers. Blogs have experienced exponential growth by enabling mass communication without requiring HTML knowledge. In fact, in 10 years the blog sites number have increased to more than 200 million (Raskino, 2007). However, it is important to notice there is need to understand further the knowledge sharing process in this setting. May authors publish their own blog and if there are neither readers nor active participants, the interest of using a blog is quite limited.

Social networking is the practice of increasing the number of business or personal contact by making connections through individuals. This system allows members of a specific site to learn about other members' skills, talents, knowledge, or preferences regardless of geographic location. The concept of social networking is of course not new, however, the Internet has provided a strong potential to extend this phenomenon beyond the usual connections through a Web-based community. Popular Web sites dedicated to social networking include Myspace, Hi5, twitters and Facebook. Professional examples dedicated to social networks include LinkedIn, XING, and Viadeo. These later sites are said to create business opportunities by enhancing communication among employees, customers who can learn about each other's background such as undertaken contact information, education, employment history, employment opportunities, and so forth.

Social bookmarking allows users to manage, store, organize, and search bookmarks of web pages. The bookmarks can be public, private, or shared only with a specific people or a given community, or the public. Social bookmark services allow users to organize their bookmarks online with informal tags instead of the traditional browser-based system of folders. Therefore, authorized people can view these bookmarks chronologically, by category or tags, or via a search engine. An interesting additional feature relies on the possibility to comment online, annotate or rate on bookmarks. Some social book markings provide web feeds allowing subscribers to become aware of creation, tagging, and saving of new bookmarks by other users. Example includes Flickrs and Delicious.

There are many tools that are available; however, it is important to understand the need of the Web 2.0 users and what type of limitation are encountered while using for instance social software tools.

2.2 Social computing software tools

Web 2.0 does also encompass "lightweight computing tools" which are becoming a new social computing trend of easy-to-use software (Parameswaran and Whinston, 2007). The software is mainly developed and made available for free by the open source community (e.g. Google, 2007). Examples are Ajax (i.e. JavaScript, XML), Python, Perl and MySQL. These software tools have attracted users with limited computer qualifications into application development, and we observe a shift towards increased grassroots participation and the emergence of situational applications based upon ad-hoc software needs and the perpetual beta of quick released (Cherbakov et al. 2007). Furthermore, interoperability facilitates combination of individual modules of functionalities that are easy to add, advance and reuse. By combining different applications across websites, users create popular mashups in a new context (Floyd et al. 2007). This "perpetual beta" principle of quick software releases does not apply rigorous systems development methods and represents a challenge towards the traditional system development cycle with seldom releases (Neff and Stark, 2003).

2.3 The users of Web 2.0

More and more studies highlight that the young generation is more inclined to use new information communication technologies.

With the expansion of computer technologies, the concepts of Digital Natives and Digital Immigrants have emerged (Prensky, 2001). Digital Natives are individuals who were born and grew up during the era of the Web, in which instant online access, instant communication with multiple peer groups are part of their thinking mode. Computers, mobile phones, and video gaming are part of their lives. Digital Immigrants were born and grew up before this era; thus, these technologies and concepts are not native to them. Individuals belong either to Digital Native or to Digital Immigrant groups (Prensky, 2001). Digital native have a more intuitive potential than digital immigrant to adopt quickly what Web 2.0 offer (Phifer, 2008). See figure 1. However, motivation of using Web 2.0 technologies is the decisive element.

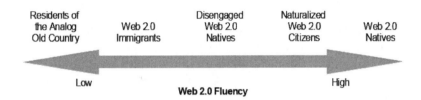

Figure 1: Spectrum of Web 2.0 fluency (Phifer, 2008)

For a successful deployment and use of Web 2.0 technologies, it is crucial to categorize the Web 2.0 users in order for enterprises to understand how to deal with employees, customers. Psychographics are essential, because they relate to the user's lifestyle, interests, aspirations and attitudes towards the use of tool such blogs, wiki, and social networks. It is not the age of the person that determines the categories but rather the people inclination to use Web 2.0 technologies (Zhiyuan, Meiyan, Yang, & Shao, 2009).

One manifestation and application of Web 2.0 in the business domain refers to the concept of Enterprise 2.0.

3   Web 2.0 in organizations-Enterprise 2.0

With the growing recognition that solely technologies have not fully delivered their promises to improve business performances (Rigby & Bilodeau, 2007), academic and practitioners have shifted their focus on solving "non technological issues" related to practices, cultures, and organizational changes (Allen, 2008). Amongst different business processes, Knowledge sharing process within and across organisations play an important role in fostering the competiveness of enterprises. Knowledge sharing process is considered as a challenging task, difficult to nurture within an organization.

It requires pro-social behaviour through social processes, for example by cultivating a sense of community.

The persistent quest to foster collaboration has led strategist's people to adopt emerging technologies supporting new networked business structures. Web 2.0, Social software, could become one of the answers for improving the way people work together and to address some of the knowledge sharing challenges.

Close studies looking at the use of Web 2.0 communities show that knowledge sharing is the fundamental nature of such approaches. For example, strong user's participations have created the recognized success of some Web sites such as Wikipedia Ebay or Amazon.

With expanding capability to connect people and the need to enable corporate knowledge sharing, it is important to provide a platform allowing many tools to be selected from. Every organisation has their own business requirements and therefore, it is important to tailor this social technological platform (Carla O'Dell, 2008).

Hence, it is crucial to understand the Web 2.0 concept, how a new breed of open, networked organization—the Enterprise 2.0 and the Intranet 2.0 is emerging and why nowadays it is gaining attention (Tapscott, 2006a, Tredinnick, 2006). The main focus is on networking, communication, communities of practices and collaborative platforms.

In the following we will elaborate on these trends to determine the potential role of Web 2.0.

3.1   Enterprise 2.0: A new way to do business

The term "Enterprise 2.0", E2.0 describes a collection of organizational and IT practices that help organizations establish flexible work models, visible knowledge-sharing practices, and higher levels of community participation. An additional interesting feature of E2.0 is the "mashup" - a website or web application that uses content from more than one source to create a completely new service.

E2.0 refers to the use of social software in order to improve knowledge sharing and foster collaboration between companies, employees, theirs customers, and partners. To illustrate this approach, Tapscott (2006a) introduce "the term of wikinomics to describe an economy in which companies are gaining competitive advantage by successfully managing a trust-based relationships with external collaborators and customers" (Johnston, 2007; Tapscott, 2006a). The last decade has seen a clear evolution toward a networked enterprises concept as a means for companies to be more competitive. Figure 2 illustrates the evolution from Web 1.0 to Enterprise 2.0.

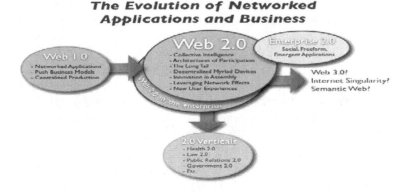

Figure 2: Evolution of networked enterprises (Hinchcliffe, 2007)

The growing adoption of E2.0 is dictated by the need to capitalize knowledge and to retain the corporate knowledge assets through a well thought human resource strategies and competence based management. In addition, the pressure on firms to innovate has forced firms to look for ways to improve their business performances. E2.0 represents a new paradigm for strategic collaboration and corporate knowledge sharing.

There is no doubt that knowledge sharing initiatives coupled with collaboration efforts are the best strategy to address the needs to retain people and reach performance goals. Although Enterprise 2.0 seems to bring the right answer, it is necessary to examine what are the barriers and limitation of Web 2.0.

3.2 New organizational forms

Recently, new organizational forms have emerged consisting of flatter, and more decentralized organizational structures compared to the traditional hierarchy. For instance, the hierarchic organizational form represents contradictory features and consists of emerging networks and temporary work teams where an improvised work style is dominating (Kellogg et al. 2006).

Moreover, researchers have interpreted organizations as a "community of communities of practice" (Brown and Duguid 1991), as social communities (Kogut and Zander 1992; Teigland 2003), or as social collectives and 'knowledge systems' (Holzner and Marx 1979). In the same vein, Contractor et al.(2006) argue that the evolving networking form is the organization.

The shift towards new organizational forms is in the practitioner-oriented literature referred to as the emergence of the Enterprise 2.0. Table 2 depicts the differences between traditional organizational forms and the heterarchic form that has similarities with the Enterprise 2.0 approach.

Table 2: Comparison of traditional and new organizational forms (Kellogg et al. 2006; Tapscott, 2007)

Organizational Dimensions	Enterprise 1.0 Hierarchical	Enterprise 2.0 Heterarchic
Form of organizing	Permanent hierarchy	Temporary work teams Networked
Decision authority	Centralized	Decentralized
Accountability	Fixed, top-down	Shifting, distributed
Division of labor and roles	Stable, specialized	Dynamic, blurred
Boundaries	Clearly specified, persistent	Fuzzy and permeable
Work process	Routine work, standardized, rule-based	Improvised, flexible, participative
Direction	Management commands	Self-managing
Individual motivation	Satisfy superiors	Achieve team goals
Learning	Specific skills	Broader competencies
Composition	Homogenous	Heterogeneous
Performance criteria	Established, singular	Emergent, multiple
Watchword	Stability, inertia	Speed, adaptability

Scholars suggest that new organization forms such as the heterarchy which represents a post-bureaucratic organizational form are more prepared for adapting effectively to new conditions of volatility and virtual spaces compared to traditional forms. Heterarchy is as well defined by David Stark as 'an emergent organizational form with distinctive network properties and multiple organizing principles' (Stark 2001).

To keep up with the dynamic environment, some firms are experimenting with dynamic strategy such as the perpetual beta approach, and forms of organizing that are more open, interconnected and adaptive (Ciborra, 1996; Neff & Stark, 2003).

4   Web 2.0 implications

It is recognized among the Practitioners that focusing only on technologies will not insure the success of Web 2.0 deployment. E2.0 could have happen even without technologies due to the fact that it is a socially-driven evolution that did not originate from a technology push nor from a demand pull (AAIM, 2008). Hence, adopting E2.0 is not about using others software tools but rather means that people have to reconsider their business routine by incorporating the collaborative paradigm in their daily work. Organizational dimension should be considered by fostering change management strategy while trying to implement new technology. Understanding organizational challenges means understanding the E2.0 adoption barriers, which identify the critical success factors.

The penetration of new technologies in the workplace has generated new type of issues and challenges. For example, selection and adoption of technology is a complex process that is based on a number of alternatives including technological choices, perceived benefits, cost based models and organizational strategies. However technology itself needs adaptation to organizational goals and strategies (Laulmann, Nadler, & O'Farrell, 1991).

Motivations for technology use are both intrinsic and extrinsic. Adaptability of technology to user needs, user confidence, and motivation to its adoption are key factors to understand. Kanter's has identified five characteristics of successful technology adoption, the five Fs -: **F**ocused, **F**ast, **F**lexible, **F**riendly, and **F**un (Kanter, 1990).

Dias (2002) identified three motivation factors for using technology, namely; perceived usefulness, perceived ease of use, and perceived enjoyment. He argues that "information technology implementation is an intervention we make in order to improve the effectiveness and efficiency of a socio-technical system" (Dias, 2002).

The deployment of novel Web 2.0 tools requires understanding the factors that will facilitate or inhibit the full adoption of their use in the workplace. It is important to examine some of the organizational issues that E2.0 must face such as governance, culture, leadership, incentive schemes, and value capture.

One factor related to the organizational culture arises from the fact that some organizations do not promote extensive collaboration and knowledge sharing outside their project teams. Thus, the Web 2.0 deployment is a challenging task.

Another factor common in many industries (e.g., manufacturing's, aerospace, automation) is the generation gap. Workforces in these sectors are aging and belong mainly to the digital immigrant group. Hence, it is challenging for some of them to use or see a need for social software in their daily work.

5 Conclusion

During the past few years, there has been a growing interest in social software under the name of Web2.0 for both the business world and the academic communities. Web2.0 represents the revolution that is happening since more and more users are transforming from passive consumers status to active participants.

However, technological innovations are not magic bullets, and will not provoke organizational change by just being deployed. Enterprise 2.0 technologies must be introduced into a dynamic environment that participants can see value in. This can be done by taking into accounts human and social contexts and providing appropriate management visioning of the future.

Just as organizations are beginning to grapple with the potential of Web 2.0 and E2.0, there are more opportunities being developed. At this point, there is a concept that looks to be the most promising and that is gaining a large amount of interest (Peter Burkhardt, 2009). The concept refers to the Semantic Web that should be understood as a means for machines to be able to understand, relate, and compile information without human intervention. This could be the starting point for the Web3.0.

References

AAIM (2008). Enterprise 2.0: Agile, Emergent & Integrated. *MarketIQ . Intelligence quartely.*

Ahonen, H., Engeström, Y., & Virkkunen, J. (2000). Knowledge Management – The second generation: Creating competencies within and between work communities in the Competence Laboratory. In A. Malhotra (Ed.), *Knowledge Management and Virtual Organizations* (pp. 282-305). London: Idea Group Publishing.

Alavi, M. (2000). Managing organizational knowledge. In R. W. Zmud (Ed.), *Framing the Domains of IT Management. Projecting the Future...Through the Past* (pp. 15-28). Cincinnati, OH: Pinnaflex Educational Resources.

Allen, P. J. (2008, 26-28 June 2008). *How Web 2.0 communities solve the knowledge sharing problem.* Paper presented at the Technology and Society, IEEE International Symposium , ISTAS Fredericton, New Brunswick, Canada.

Berners-Lee, T. (2000). *Weaving the web* (Second ed.). London: Texere Publishing Limited.

Boulos, K. M., N. , & Wheeler, S. (2007). The emerging Web 2.0 social software: an enabling suite of sociable technologies in health and health care education. *Health Information and Libraries Journal, 24, 24*, pp 2-23.

Carla O'Dell (2008). *Web 2.0 and Knowledge Management.*

Castells, M. (2000). Material for an exploratory theory of the network Society. *The British Journal of Sociology, 51*(1), 5-24.

Ciborra, C. U. (1996). The Platform Organization: Recombining Strategies, Structures, and Surprises. *Organization Science, 7*(2), 103-118.

Dias, D. D. S. (2002). Motivation for Using Information Technology. In E. Szewczak & C. Snodgrass (Eds.), *Human Factors in Information Systems* (pp. 55-60): IGI Press.

Gibbons, M., Limoges, C., Nowotny, H., Schwartzman, S., Scott, P., & Trow, M. (1994). *The new production of knowledge: The dynamics of science and research in contemporary societies.* London: Sage Publications.

Gotta, M. (2007). *Enterprise 2.0: Collaboration and Knowledge Management Renaissance.* Midvale, Utah.

Grossman, M., & McCarthy, R. V. (2007). Web 2.0: Is the Enterprise Ready for the Adventure. *Issues in Information Systems, 8*(2), 180-185.

Harrison, R., & Thomas, M. (2009). Identity in Online Communities: Social Network-ing Sites and Language Learning *International Journal of Emerging Technologies & Society 7*(2), pp: 109 - 124.

Hinchcliffe, D. (2007). The state of Enterprise 2.0. *ZDNET*. Retrieved from http://blogs.zdnet.com/Hinchcliffe/?p=143

Huysman, M., de Wit, D., Ackerman, M. S., Pipek, V., & Wulf, V. e. (2003). A Critical Evaluation of Knowledge Management Practices *Sharing expertise: Beyond knowledge management* (pp. 27-55): Cambridge and London:

MIT Press.

Jennex, M. E. (2008). Exploring System Use as a Measure of Knowledge Manage-ment Success. *journal of Organizational & End User Computing, 20*(1), 50-63.

Johnston, K. (2007). Folksonomies, Collaborative Filtering and e-Business: is Enter-prise 2.0 One Step Forward and Two Steps Back? *5*(4), 411-418

Kanter, R. M. (1990). *When Giants Learn To Dance*: Free Press.

Kellogg, K. C., Orlikowski, W. J., & Yates, J. (2006). Life in the Trading Zone: Structur-ing Coordination Across Boundaries in Postbureaucratic Organizations. *Organi-zation Science, 17*(1), 22-44.

Laulmann, E., Nadler, G., & O'Farrell, B. (1991). Designing for technological Change: People in the Process. In N. R. C. National Academy of Engineering and Com-mission on Behavioral and Social Sciences and Education (Ed.), *People and Technology in the Workplace* (pp. 1-14). Washington, DC: The National Academ-ic Press.

Mann, J. (2007). *Why Knowledge Management Is No Longer on the Gartner Hype Cycles* (No. G00151237): Gartner Research.

McAfee, A. (2006). Enterprise 2.0: The Dawn of Emergent Collaboration. *MIT Sloan Management Review, 47*(3), 21-28.

Musser, J., & O'Reilly, T. (2006). Web 2.0. Principles and Best Practices

Neff, G., & Stark, D. (2003). Permanently Beta: Responsive organization in the In-ternet era. In P. N. Howard & S. Jones (Eds.), *Society Online: The Internet in Context* (pp. 173-188). Thoasand Oaks, CA: Sage Publications.

O'Reilly, T. (2005). What is Web 2.0? Retrieved Oct 20, 2005

Peter Burkhardt (2009). Social Software Trends in Business:. Retrieved from http://www.igi-global.com/downloads/excerpts/8352.pdf

Phifer, G. (2008). Web 2.0 User Categories: Beyond Digital Natives and Digital Im-migrants. *ID Number: G00164326*. Retrieved from http://www.gartner.com/AnalystBiography?authorId=10250

Prensky, M. (2001). Digital Natives, Digital Immigrants Retrieved from http://www.marcprensky.com/writing/prensky%20-%20digital%20natives,%20digital%20immigrants%20-%20part1.pdf

Raskino, M. (2007). *In 2008, Enterprise Web 2.0 Goes Mainstream* (No. Gartner G00153218).

Redmiles, D., & Wilensky, H. (2008). *Adoption of Web 2.0 in the Enterprise:Technological Frames of KM Practitioners and Users*. Paper presented at the Workshop for CSCW 2008. from
http://swiki.cs.colorado.edu:3232/CSCW2008-Web20/33

Rigby, D., & Bilodeau, B. (2007). *Management Tools and Trends 2007*: Bain & Company.

Sau-ling, L. (2010). Social Commerce – E-Commerce in Social Media Context. *World Academy of Science, Engineering and Technology, 72*, 39-45.

Shapiro, C., & Varian, H. R. (1999). *Information rules: a strategic guide to the network economy*. Boston: Harvard Business School Press.

Smith, D. M. (2008). Web 2.0 and Beyond: Evolving the Discussion. *Gartner, Number: G00154767*. Retrieved from
http://mslibrary/research/MktResearch/Gartner2/research/154700/154767/154767.html

Tapscott, D. (2006a). Winning with the Enterprise 2.0. Retrieved from
http://www.cob.sjsu.edu/jerrell_l/Tapscott%20on%20Collab%20Advantage.pdf

Tapscott, D. (2006b). Winning with the Enterprise 2.0

Tapscott, D. (2007). Wikinomics. Harnessing the Power of Mass Collaboration. *Enterprise 2.0 Conference presentations*

Tapscott, D., & Willams, A. (2006). *Wikinomics: How Mass Collaboration Changes Everything*. New York Penguin Group.

Tiwana, A. (2002). *The Knowledge Management Toolkit, Orchestrating IT, Strategy, and Knowledge Platforms* (2nd ed.). Upper Saddle River, NJ: Prentice Hall.

Toffler, A. (1981). *The third wave*. London: Pan books.

Tredinnick, L. (2006). Web 2.0 and Business: A pointer to the intranets of the future? *Business Information Review, 23*(4), 228-234.

Zhiyuan, F., Meiyan, X., Yang, J., & Shao, Z. (2009). *Influence Factors to Web2.0 Websites Users' Attitude and Behavioral Intention*. Paper presented at the IEEE International Conference on e-Business Engineering, Macau.

173